$1·95

Mister B.

IRVING PETITE

Published by arrangement with Doubleday & Company, Inc.
First Paperback Edition 1976

Seattle Book Company
P.O. Box 9254
Seattle, Washington 98109

TO

Mister B., who lived it—
Caroline Rogers, who inspired the telling—
And to those who respect life, in all its forms

CONTENTS

I *Birth*

He was born on a day when the wind stilled, about noon, in tall evergreen trees above his mother's den. A lid of nimbus clouds hung a dull "snow sky" overhead, above a small south waft of wind, just enough to make sounds coming from the south more distinct than those in the north, so that sound kept lapping, like slight, incoming waves, up the length of the Puget Sound country in western Washington. The human mind's eye could see sound ripples running up the map from the Oregon border, below, to the Canadian boundary, above. It was New Year's Day, 1960.

Had his mother stuck her glistering-black, pointy snoot out the oval slot of the den opening, she might have heard a rooster crow from the ranch yard several hundred feet southeastward across a large creek, or a car laboring on one of the slippery, uphill turns of Tiger Mountain Road which runs through the ranch along its southern edge. But she did not. She was preoccupied. Her body had given, in womb, pelvis, and breasts, the signs signifying birth. She waited without nature's anesthetic, hibernation—and, in fact, no mother bear in that latitude was totally asleep at such a time. In the cave her body heat made the chamber warm; snow, lipped up at the already narrow entrance until it was nearly sealed, helped to keep the heat in.

Her age made her supple; her experience, wise. She was nearly five years old, through with growing toward the 350 pounds which was to be her total weight, give or take thirty or forty pounds of berry-fat in autumn. She carried her weight well, being solidly built, and did not appear to have half the bulk of a human being of her poundage. She knew what to expect, since this was her second birthing, her first having come two Januarys past, a few days previous to her own third birthday.

Like the first, this was easy, the cubs coming within a few minutes of one another. In spite of her own heaviness, her infants weighed only eight ounces apiece. They were bare, pink-skinned, blind, and small enough, each one, to fit into the shell of a goose egg.

As they were born, she curved her head and licked the afterbirth and membrane from them, starting with their naked heads and tongue-scrubbing all the mucous first from their faces, then from their entire bodies. Their bare muzzles gave a tinny whining, while their boldly-pink nostrils opened and closed as convulsively as the gill openings of stranded fish. Their nostrils flared, tightened, twitched. They sneezed. Eyes closed, they shook their bare, indiscernibly-blonde-fuzzed knobs of heads waveringly, like newborn kittens.

Within a few minutes their mouths were suckered tightly over the topmost of her several pairs of nipples, and their pink tongues tentatively applied pressure. When they had broken away the slight stoppage at each opening, the thick, protein-rich, slightly laxative colostrum milk came.

The scents of birthing stayed in the cave, ground-hugging. No animal, not even the winter-lean bobcat passing on the trail a few feet to the west, would smell it. Outside, the day—and so, seemingly, the entire universe—remained as still as if nothing had happened . . . in a space of *pause* which could itself be felt as surely as, to the human or animal consciousness, the texture of bark travels up from finger-pads to the brain.

It was a tranquil time. The mother was well equipped by nature and by her own placid temperament for a two weeks' doze in a space bounded by a giant log above, the log's trunk extending eastward, the root ends westward, warm earth below and for a backing.

Although she was almost five years old, she had never climbed to the top of nearby Tiger Mountain, nor would she ever do so, even if she lived another decade. She would never, unless pursued beyond all expectations, move more than a few thousand feet from her own original birthing place. Her mother had disappeared when she, herself, was nearly two years old and ready to find her own mate; and her mother's "territory"—lush with spring grasses and roots, summer berries and small fruits, and rife with snug denning-places—had become her own. Her succession of dens would all encircle, within a few hundred feet, that of her own birth.

She lived at approximately eight hundred feet above sea level. Could she have suddenly been elevated to Tiger Mountain's top, twenty-six hundred feet more or less, she would have been able to see (had she also had good vision) Mount Rainier standing against the sky to the south, the stack of the Tacoma smelter to the southwest, and, to the west and north, the buildings of Seattle: the Smith Tower, the Meany Hotel. There would be ribbons of water, too: Lake Sammamish, Lake Washington, Puget Sound.

As it was, she was destined to move only a few hundred feet up or down the mountainside, lifelong. She would have a tendency to move *up*, for her inclination was to go *back* when disturbed or when seeking a fresh den site.

Her cubs had come from one darkness to a larger one where, when their eyes began to open in about two weeks, a sliver of light sifted in from under one far edge. The cubs' world, like that of a human infant, was a series of grays at first—from deep to light and back again to deep— day and night being undifferentiated and the only change in their "light environment" being a deepening or light- ening of the inverted upper lip of light that was the cave's slotted entrance.

As they grew, they became more vocal, like newborn kittens or puppies. They complained when their mother jostled them from her warm belly as she rolled over on her side or belly to sleep, leaving them, temporarily, with- out a nipple to cling to. They complained as they tried laboriously to clamber over her high side, mewling like distraught kittens.

They did not take much milk, only a few tablespoonfuls a day; but it was, at first, a continuous chore for them to draw off the colostrum milk with its properties of rich min- eral and physic. They slumbered mostly, clinging to the nipples which were blue-white islands in a jungle of coarse, black hair. When they half awoke, to drink again, they pushed and trod with their forepaws, the nails of which were hardening and becoming sharper by the hour, against the source of their nourishment, meanwhile humming an up-and-down-the-scale singsong and making the small, contented, squealing noises similar to those made by newborn piglets.

As they took more of her milk, the mother felt thirstier than she had since her retreat to the den—to sleep, but not to "hibernate"—several weeks previously. She rolled on one side, holding the cubs to her with her upper arm, and thrust her long, purplish tongue along the snow skifted up just outside the den opening.

But she craved a real drink from the tumbling, ice-cold creek veining the woods at the bottom of a ravine about eighty feet to the northwest. The water of that creek was always crystal clear, even when it was in small flood from spring or autumn rains. Tree-canopied along its entire course—from springs in a mountainous bluff a mile above, to where it met the large creek a thousand feet downstream—it ran over logs and rocks that grew moss even under water, so that the stream was virtually running on a mossy bed. How she needed a long, gullet-filling, body-easing drink!

Toward dusk, on an evening two weeks following her cubs' birth, she gently scooped them away from her breast with her forepaws, rolling them from her and piling them against the packed earth at the back of the den. The cave warmth and their own body heat, together with their silky coverings of new body hair, would keep them warm for a time. They squirmed, clutching one another tightly, and making small, sniveling noises in their half-sleep.

She flattened herself against the den floor and eased outward.

In the gray, outer-world light she sniffed for danger odors. There were none. She pushed herself on through, snugging under a nearby log whose underside scratched her back luxuriously; climbed between it and a third log; nosed through a small thicket of salal bushes; and stood upright on a deserted logging road that had, during the past twenty years, become a travel route for animals. She could hear and smell the creek, and she pushed forward toward it, making little noise. Another animal, a few feet away on the trail, would have sensed rather than seen her: she was merely a shadow passing.

Sixty to eighty feet overhead, in the tops of hemlock and Douglas-fir trees where there was still a ribbon of light, she heard the faint, sad, paternostering voices of a family of five Canadian jays as they quibbled about a roosting place for the night. Otherwise, silence. She moved on down to the creek.

When she drank, carefully keeping her feet out of the water, the sensation was that belonging to one of her life's climaxes: luxurious, replenishing, fulfilling. She stood back, nose lifted, grasped the earth firmly with all four feet, and shook herself hugely, like a horse shaking out his whole hide after a roll in the dust. She literally bathed in the icy air. All the creases straightened out; the small frets fell away; the world was hers!

When she returned to the den, the cubs sensed her feeling of renewed well-being, and their own world felt more secure. Living in the den was, for them, like living inside a shell a child puts to his ear at the seashore: a muffled roar of silence.

They were laved continually in the reassuring smell of their mother, whose glistering, long, black belly hair they clung to and tussled in. Mingled with her smell was the pungent, spice-odor of hemlock and Western-red-cedar twigs which she began snipping from nearby trees and bringing into the cave . . . dropping them outside, slipping herself in on her belly, like a shoehorn, then turning and pulling the small boughs in with her mouth. And there were also the delicious scents of the insides of logs, giving off the invisible smoke of that slow combustion called decomposition.

Just one element ever disturbed their secret world and their utter security in it. Occasionally, a thud would vibrate the ground overhead and beyond them, or there would be a rumble and a faint oily-gassy scentstream sifting into the cave. Then their mother would toss uneasily, dislodging them, and pay little attention to them even when they wailed to reattach themselves securely to their lives' mainstream. Sometimes, when she left them on her breast, the milk might still go sluggish or even dry up altogether.

And then the cubs would feel, with their entire bodies, the quickening of vibration which meant that their mother's heart was beating quickly. A vague, quickening answering beat would seize their own tiny bodies and shake them with unreasoned emotion, as a leaf turns and twists helplessly before the wind.

II *Bear Music*

On a lightly snow-skifted day, January 19, 1960, we first heard that busy, burbling, nasally pitched song which would be identified as *bear music*.

Bill, my partner, and I had bought this quarter section of rough and roughly logged-off land in 1941. Every year since, we had worked out a logging project of one kind or another, utilizing the down logs and cedar snags that had been bypassed earlier. From the cedar we split seven-foot fence posts, twenty-one-foot hop poles, shakes, rails, and grape stakes. From straight-grained fir logs, some of them five feet through, we split mine lagging. One year, from logs that had been left behind, we sawed enough rough lumber to frame, roof, and side a modern, three-bedroom house.

It pleased me to see the waste logs used. Ever since I had observed the sawing of four- to six-inch "logs" by a Shanghai sawmill, the "slab sides" sliding out, cardboard-thin, across the sidewalk, I had realized that we are immensely wealthy, even in what is considered waste. A single log left in our woods because it was pitchy, knotty, or hard to reach, would have provided that Shanghai sawmill with a week's raw material.

This year, 1960, the live hemlock trees of the ranch's most thickly timbered area were coming out to make more growing room for the Douglas fir. The hemlock, Bill had decided, was large enough to make sawed railroad ties. The tops would make eight-foot pulpwood logs. A portable sawmill, owned by a man in Yakima, was promised to us for early spring—as soon as it is possible to tow it across the large creek that runs diagonally across the property. Meanwhile, we were felling the hemlocks, limbing them, and bucking them into eighteen-foot lengths; making roads through the woods with a rented bulldozer; and dragging the logs to the millsite with the dozer and a team of black Belgian horses.

We had felled and bucked in a half-circle through thirty acres of woodland to a place where three wind-felled old-growth logs lay, their root ends slightly separate, their tops crisscrossed together about seventy feet beyond. I cut a solid chunk out of the first log: it was sound, and would make rough timbers. Bill climbed the second log and started across to the third, which had been down for so long that a fifty-foot cedar tree had grown up with its own roots entwined in the upended roots of the down tree.

"Listen!" Bill said.

Standing quietly on the second, snow-crusted log, we heard a noise as of several kittens meowling in one of their moods of half-unease, half-hunger, or play. The sounds came from a dark, low, oval opening under the third log. The opening was not large—a slot rather than a hole—approximately fourteen inches at its widest point from ground to log. The earth was smooth before it, where an animal had many times gone in and out on its belly.

While we stood, the sounds turned to a hubble-bubble-pipe-like burbling, beginning on a high note and sliding down to a level pitch, which was held. Then the noises of fiercely industrious nursing began—perhaps amplified through the log, in the still woods.

Bobcat kits, I thought from the meowling noise. But what about the burbling? I had never heard kittens (or anything else, for that matter) make such a noise. It must be one of the secret voices of bobcats, private to the family den. I marveled at how close these wild things were to our houses —merely across a pasture and creek and a few hundred feet into the woods. It was a place we had traveled by many times, for an unused logging road, grown up to tough-leafed salal bushes, bordered the root ends of the logs. We had split fence posts from cedar logs nearby. And in the previous autumn a youngster and I had traversed the forest floor all around these logs, gathering Douglas-fir cones to sell by the gunnysackful for seed.

The nursing stopped. There were music noises again. Then squeaks, something like the sounds baby minks make— but it was the wrong season for them. Then spits like bobcat kits! And singing again.

It was like a musical rainbow encompassing the whole scale. At first I had thought it to be one-noted, but it was not; it went weirdly up and down, m-mmm-m-mum-mim-mumm-mim-mmm-m, on different notes.

We slid down near the dim opening in order to hear better.

The burbling ceased and a caterwauling began as several— it sounded like three, four, or five—small bodies were dislodged by an uneasy movement of the mother. "We'll have to leave these logs alone till summer," I whispered.

Silence below. We were about to leave when we heard

a subterranean, adult growl. Bill dangled his cap down by the opening and we waited for a bobcat claw to swipe at it.

Instead, there was the quick dart of a pointy, indiarubber-tipped nose, two alert, dime-sized, jet eyes, and a low forehead . . . and a simultaneous expulsion of sound: *Fwhoof!*

I'd wondered if bears did hibernate. Now I knew, even as I made a fast retreat. Bill dropped his cap and it fell where the mother bear's head had been before she retracted it, leaving ample evidence for the myth-makers. I could hear them proclaim, pointing: "Look where a bear got a man! That's all she left, not even bones!"

She was wide awake but did not then, or in the months after she left the den for the nearby woods, institute pursuit—in spite of her advantages of strength, speed, and three hundred to four hundred pounds of weight. Individual bears are as individually different as any other animals, including humans. This mother, we found, was patient, or tolerant, or timid almost beyond belief, and in the winter and spring months shared the woods with us without once making a threatening move or even a defensive one, beyond growling when cornered in her cave—which, we discovered after she had left it, had but one entrance. We had heard and read (and were vigorously assured, particularly by city dwellers) of mother-bear ferocity, but this particular mother just did not show, or had not developed, the trait.

Returning to the woods in the following days we passed the cave in order to leave mushy-ripe apples—which the mother took—and dried beet pulp (a cow feed)—which she left untouched. Sometimes we heard a hollow groan, like the ghost in Hamlet, but mostly she was as silent as the snowy woods of winter. But the little ones were vocal, almost every time, and we thought that they must hew to their den song day-long.

What did the mother eat, outside of our small, unseasonal offerings, we wondered.

We saw that she had brought six- to nine-inch boughs of redolent Western red cedar (*Thuja plicata*) into the den. Perhaps the fresh greenery served as roughage for her and /or pacifiers for the cubs, for after Mister B. came to us I observed him to have a special liking for cedar boughs, which he chewed without swallowing.

Cedar boughs the mother could gather by sliding out through the den opening and climbing the pole-straight, papery-barked cedar tree a few feet away. Later, in January and early February, with snow still on the ground, she carried in hemlock branches, with needles and small cones intact, from trees which we had felled before we knew of the den and whose tops reached nearby. Hemlock needles, unlike the rounded foliage of cedar, are sharp. Autumn winds had long ago blown the seeds from the cones—seeds which would have been slight provender at any rate, since it takes three hundred thousand of them to make a pound. Perhaps the mother merely craved variety in her den's rug, for neither needles nor cones seemed to be a likely food.

Active as she was, she did not enjoy even the "deep or fitful cold-weather sleep" that I was to read about later in an article explaining that bears are not true hibernators. "Our" bear family rarely slept at all, and in daily walks past the den we heard the cubs caterwauling, bubbling, yowling, and making other peaceful domestic noises such as we had never known bears to be capable of. Their farthest-out noise was a low-pitched buzzling, like that you hear just before disturbed hornets or yellow jackets burst forth from a concealed nest. Only once or twice were they utterly silent—napping, or perhaps alerted to an alien presence outside.

They sang with great gusto for such small bodies, for while Kodiak bear cubs (for instance, those born at Woodland Park Zoo in Seattle on January 14, a few days before we first heard ours) may weigh one-and-a-half pounds at birth, black bears weigh only about eight ounces, as much as a cup of water. At birth they are about the same size as puppies of a small breed such as beagles, and more vulnerable. The day we first heard them in the den, yowling, "skritching," and burbling, they were less than three weeks old—so they must be practically born singing.

The vocalizing did not, apparently, draw predators such as coyotes or bobcats into the cave. If it brought them near, in curiosity, they must have received the same greeting given Bill's cap—which stayed where it had fallen, only sliding a bit farther down the slight incline at the cave front as the mother went in and out over it.

Just hearing bear voices made the logging project seem worthwhile to me after all. The monetary success of the venture depended upon whether or not the railroad-company buyers, optimistic *before* the hemlock ties were sawed, would buy them once the project was completed. I sensed that they would buy, then, only at a downgraded price or not at all. Also, I had always prided myself on following to the letter Thoreau's precept to beware of any enterprise which required new clothes, and this one required new boots, or surely *would* when I came entirely through my soles into the snow. The project would "release" the Douglas firs to more sunlight and space, encouraging them to more rapid growth and improving our private forest. This, although long-term, was all to the good. But the work itself was much too steady, requiring rising in the dark, choring, getting to the woods just before daylight, returning to choke down a quick lunch, and then back again until dark. It cramped the soul. It tied a wet, unappetizing (even agonizing) knot in one end of the line the spirit runs out on. It was like prison, an abasement. (In my mind, at least, it was these things, for everything blooms or fades in the mind, and to a prisoner in a cell it might have been heaven on earth, at least for the first few days following release.)

The hemlock logs made pink stains on the snow where their bark rubbed off on the rocks underneath, until the skid trails bled their full length from woods to sawmill site. As any human heart will, as long as it can feel and when it has burdens which it cannot "fell and buck," my heart had similar streaks upon it that winter. A young probationer, who had once lived with me and attended Issaquah High School, was currently on a cross-country race to Florida and back on someone else's credit card, trying to "shake" his conscience and succeeding only in tobogganing himself toward the state reformatory. Nothing said or done could alter his course. But in the woods, nevertheless, I strung out my own invisible blood trails while the hemlock logs bled visibly and the vapor trails of jet planes made their whorled or straight-waked chalk marks on the evening sky.

But the singing bears, from the day we first heard them, made life possible.

From that time on, we shared the woods; we went to them, as it were, companioned. The mother bear was a presence *felt*. Even when I was not thinking about the bear family, she was a thing noted by the senses, not quite up to the level of conscious recognition . . . like a feeling or a fact between longtime lovers which is *known* but which will never need to be said.

Once when I went back to retrieve a choker or a tool at that time of slightly after dusk and before total dark when the earth ceases even to breathe for a space, I heard the mother bear slanting past on a slight hillside without actually seeing her. There was just the sound of her moving. It was a *moving past,* not retreat and not pursuit; and I think that she was on an errand of her own without even knowing I had returned to the woods—or perhaps she knew me as a *moving-past* presence, too.

It was as one hears, afar off, the sound of the Western Ocean while one is still in deep woods near its margin and cannot see the combers rolling in from China. It was a reassuring, not a spooky sound, giving a feeling of another being present in the deep woods, her almost-silence matching my own. There is something about the woods, especially at dusk or when first light slants in through the trees like light coming through the high, stained-glass windows of an empty cathedral, that awes all animals—human or otherwise— to a respectful silence.

So, out of silence and even grief, that winter came, as it always will if one waits long enough and endures, singing. In my mind it rhymed: What is so rare as the song of the bear. And out of the singing would emerge acquaintanceship with one of the authors of that song, Mister B.

III *Mister B. Appears*

The trail from the den darkened with travel in early March. Claw marks deepened on nearby cedar trees, particularly the one standing arrow-straight a few feet to the west of the den opening. It bore bark slashes like the marks on a much-used utility pole ripped by the spikes of linemen's climbers. But the scars were not as radical, and did not confirm the contention of some that bears ruin trees by climbing them.

Bears often split deciduous shrub trees, like mountain ash and cascara, in climbing for the fruit; but it would take bear travel such as I have never seen to ruin a well-started evergreen tree. Our horses ruined some young firs and Scotch pines which we had planted, by standing over them and using them for "itching" posts; in the deep woods, porcupines stripped some of the young cedars which had been so tardy in starting that they never would have developed to adulthood in any event; but the bears left marks, nothing more. In the cascara thickets the upper limbs hung every which way, like straws of much-badgered brooms, and sometimes the trees were split down the middle and died. But the true encroachers were men, even with the cascaras;

their frequent practice in harvesting the medicinal bark, to be dried and sold at local feed stores during the spring and early summer, was to kill the trees by girdling them up to the height they could easily reach. The remainder of the bark they left: a total waste. Because they were usually trespassing and wished to make no noise, they also neglected to saw or chop the trees off at the base. A cascara tree cut off six to ten inches above the ground will sprout and grow new trees; one left standing stands black and mute for years, a testimony to man's greed.

A few chosen visitors to the ranch we took for a walk into the woods and past the den, letting them share the spine-tickling sounds of bear-singing. Haruko Nelson, the Japanese wife of a radioman we knew, giggled delightedly and whispered: "I'm going to write to my mother about this; she won't believe it."

"The mother bear will take them for a walk on the first sunny day," Bill said.

I do not know from what hidden well of intuition he fished this fact, but it was so. The first moderately sunny day, March 19, he traveled past the den and thought it to be empty. He was sure of it when, the following day, he saw the apple he had left the day before untouched. Two days later, with the logs all on the rollaway above the millsite, we ceased logging operations. Bill went to Seattle on business, and I drove the pickup into the woods above the den and began working into fence posts some of the cedar logs that were not suitable for sawing into boards.

"Nameless," the white cocker-type dog that someone had dropped off up the road that same January and who had become the most loyal among five dogs on the ranch, was with me. She made exploratory side trips, but mostly she was within a few feet of me. About noon I shut off the chain saw and straightened up to sunlight that did not warm but was like a chilling hand upon my forehead and flanks. Down at a limby brush pile below the road Nameless was making an irregular, yapping circle. Squirrel caught off-base with no escape tree, I thought.

In answer came a horrible, high-pitched, continued screaming as of an animal in mortal agony. Nameless stood, stump-tail rigid, or rushed in and out at the source of the noise, her lips drawn back in a snarl over her Pekingese-looking front teeth. From the sounds, the animal she had discovered appeared to me to be a member of the cat family. Or could a porcupine make such a noise? I wondered. A few weeks earlier a hawk or owl had taken a young rabbit in the woods above and the usually silent rabbit had, in death's clutch, shrieked with the same desperation of whatever now crouched in the brush pile. But this was not a rabbit's voice. Whatever it was, it wasn't trapped, unless perhaps by the brush, for we had never set traps except —and then, ineffectually—for coyotes when we first came here in the 1940s.

Whatever it is, I thought, it will slide away when Nameless quits haunting it. I called her back and resumed work, but before long she was back, yapping at the brush pile. Occasionally the object of her attentions roused and answered with an unearthly screeching. I slid down quietly until I could see a small black puff of fur among the brush. A baleful, round, black eye opened and stared toward me: a bear cub! The eye closed; the bundle of fur, perfectly silent now, quivered all over.

This is where his walk with mother bear ended, I thought. She can't be far away and certainly she has heard him by now; if I leave the woods, she will come back to round him up; so I called Nameless and drove back to the other side of the creek.

I'd seen plenty of black bears, large ones and growing-sized, retreating—with varying degrees of rapidity—in the two decades we'd lived on the ranch. But the first black bear I ever saw coming toward me was the caterwauling infant, a "reject" cub, following Nameless, the "reject" dog. I was splitting cedar shakes in the front field when the procession of two came home. I dropped the mallet and froe and knelt on the damp ground before the cub. My warmth and size probably half-approximated motherness; anyway, the wailing cub tumbled forward and, grabbing hold with front paws around the arm of my old olive-drab knit sweater, climbed up and began nuzzling my neck and making the nursing sounds which we had heard from the den.

He had that fearlessness toward humans which many young animals, incompletely trained by their parents, show. His front claws clung to my sweater's neck; his body trembled all over with cold and hunger, instilling in me, immediately, that protectiveness which passes through one, as definitely as an electric current, when something or someone, smaller and more helpless even than one's self, shows trust. "Comfort me. Feed me. Let me trust you." It is the most basic call known to man.

The geode you saw as a child was the most spectacular one of your life because it was the only one you ever really did *see*. And so I saw the cub, from fuzzy head to agate-shiny claws, and on down to his tail, like a mashed-flat, cut-off whisk broom, one much-used and reduced to about half-length. He was all claws and ears and wide-open mouth shaped like the one you glimpse under an elephant's trunk.

He had black, round, lashless eyes—bare-rimmed, too, like an elephant's. But he was only about as big as a drinking gourd with juglike ears—or a robin's nest with a hump on it. When I cupped one hand under his hindquarters, he seemed to weigh about four pounds.

I called Ellen, a neighbor who had spent all her life close to nature's story as written in the woods, along streams, and on the mountainside, in order to have someone with whom to share this treasure, for the miracle of life is nowhere so poignant as in an infant being. We warmed a pan of milk and I dislodged Mister B. from his clawhold on my neck. I set him on the thick-pile living-room rug, and while he clung to my forearm I gave him milk by the spoonful.

Suddenly he gave a shudder of warmth, security, and fullness, and fell asleep. We put him on an old sweater in a basket that had held Christmas fruit. Then we went back across the creek to be sure that he was the brush-pile cub, and to see if we could locate the mother. When we returned, we could hear him "waaahing" from clear across the field: "The baby's awake."

He was standing up in the basket, bawling. He opened his pink-lined mouth with a hunger "Wah!" and his eyes glittered.

He drank again, until he was on the outside of more than a cup of milk, spoonful by spoonful. I could feel his belly distending against the wrist he straddled, for he had consumed about a fifth of his entire body weight. From then on he slept in his basket straight through until morning, with only a look up and over the basket edge when Bill got home.

The following day, after feeding him, I left for the woods. Bill was already there, making final adjustments at the sawmill site, preparatory to sawing. Later, he came down to where I was working, his face alight. "Come on!" he said.

I followed him up the road past the rollaway, then in at an angle to a side hill that faced south and caught all the sun. It was a place where evergreen trees had thickly hedged the road but where the trees had grown poorly at hill center.

"Look!" There, upright as a brand-new Teddy bear squatted on a charcoal-covered log, sat a near-perfect replica of Mister B. This one looked slightly better fed, however.

This second little cub on the hillside doddered in the pale sunlight, half-chilled, half-asleep—and totally unafraid, or else too numb to entertain fear. I realized, later, that it did not even see us, save perhaps as wavering shadows.

After looking our fill we slid away with that silent respect which woods and woods-things instill in humans. On the road I asked: "How did you find her?" (I felt about the second cub as "her," for some reason.)

"Making that *waah*," Bill said. "She was really screeching."

She was only about 150 feet in a straight line from where Mister B. had been when Nameless discovered him, and only a few dozen feet above the millsite.

Later, we returned with a flat cardboard container with some of the bakery rolls that had come in it, and slices of apple. The Teddy bear still doddered in silence, opening its eyes, then closing them again. She did not move, except to shiver. Bill set the food down on the log a few feet from her. Then we heard the mother coming back through the brush on the hillside above. Very possibly there was one more cub up in that direction and the mother was moving them uphill in relays; we never knew.

The experience indicated to us the fallacy in thinking, as

woodsmen and innocents alike do, that bear mothers are always fiercely protective, terrifically jealous animals, quick to go after and to rescue their cubs in danger. Actually, they may purposefully abandon their cubs, and I always thought of this one as "the mother who left home."

Getting to know Mister B. better, I did not blame her so much. She had possibly had enough of his sharp claws, teething bites, and the constant insistence of the little beast for milk that she probably did not have in sufficient quantity. She had been restless, undoubtedly, even before we found the cave—because of the sounds of the chain saw, trees thudding to earth, the diesel motor of the bulldozer, the sound and scent of the dog—and certainly most nervous after we discovered the one-entrance den. The effect of being more wakeful than usual had probably used some of her body energy that normally would have gone into making milk. Nervous strain may have dried up her milk flow, too. And even our attempts to be helpful with food may have had poor effect, for apples, even when mushy-ripe, are not the best of milk-producing foods.

From meeting the other, doddering little hillside-cub, one could deduce that it had an utterly different personality from that of Mister B., and this may well have made the mother's decision about which one to leave behind extremely simple. "She" of the hillside was shy, calm, and "good." She wailed, true, but she also had the good sense to shut up when an alien shadow appeared. She had that retiring nature so necessary to social success and, possibly, to pleasing a mother bear.

I figured that Mister B. had clawed and bitten his mother unmercifully throughout the first two and a half months of his life, and that she had batted at him nervously, as at a huge horsefly on her bosom. And finally, when she saw him tangled in the brush pile, she had peered back and "said," with sentiments similar to those spoken by a seaman to the bos'n halfway to China on one of the ships I had sailed: "To heck weeth thees! I queet!"

IV *Bear Essentials*

Mister B. took to the house as to a second cave. Warmth and food were his bare essentials. The food part, easily accomplished, gave way to his need for warmth, perpetually, and house warmth alone would not do it. He did not ever sleep on the hot-air registers from the furnace as domestic creatures did. He did not loll on the hearth, basking before the fireplace fire, in the spot which had been preferred by a black-tailed deer we reared.

No, there was only one kind of warmth for Mister B.: close, personal, physical contact. When the physical host was present, he clutched, clung to, "talked" to, nuzzled, and nudged it. When the host was absent, he slept fitfully in a pile of old sweaters in my workroom closet—or bellowed for his warm friend.

He required *closeness*. This begins in the cave when he lies upon the mother's recumbent form almost constantly for the first two and a half months of his life, so that there is always a larger warmness, a safe harbor of hot, warm, furry, arm-enveloping security for him.

It was easy for me to respond with closeness, for I feel it, too, with all things loved. But it was not a smothering-

34

mothering on my part, for the day's chores did not allow for that, nor did my disposition. I let him crawl and bawl.

The most difficult thing to adjust to was his eternal nuzzling. He had the animal world's most expressive lips. Orally tactile, he was forever lipping and tonguing everything in his universe, getting its measure through taste and lip-feel. Later, this would encompass everything from dandelion down to cottonwood fluff to sand by the creek and rocks on the road, caterpillars, and chicken feathers, but for the present it was confined mainly to food and his hosts' bodies.

And here he raised a kind of havoc. When he was done with his milk dish and had dried his arm fur and licked up what was spilled on the kitchen tile, he was far from done with the motions of eating. Now came digesting and dreaming. He climbed a leg or clambered onto a lap, and began nuzzling at a forearm, underarm, cheek, or chin. Under the chin was his favorite spot at first; later, when he was more adult, it became the forearm. While he nursed, tugging with his lips and folded tongue at the skin, he kept up one of the mumbling-muttering noises we had heard emanating from the cave: mmmmm-mummm-mim-mumm-mnnim. It went on interminably, rising and falling in a rhythm of its own, perhaps one coordinated to the rising and falling of mother bear's Brobdingnagian breast.

He burrowed in; his nails hung on, not "working" like a kitten's, but clutching; usually he closed his eyes. I suppose that he was back in the world of cave darkness, warmth, and total security—had moved himself back to the time before rejection and the cold-hunger misery of the hours spent alone while his mother went on toward the mountain.

He did not wish, ever, to return to that time. With teeth, claws, and screeches he made it evident. He was all right as long as he was tolerated, nuzzling at an inside-forearm or neck; but when he was dislodged, ah, that was a different matter! He took it as a personal rejection, as a danger to survival, it seemed—and would dig in with his claws and then take a quick bite at the skin area he had been nuzzling. With the bite went a horrible, high-pitched, continuous squalling, so fierce one could hear it all over the mountain.

His yowling unhappiness at being left alone opened the doors for him and when we were working near the house he was free to follow. No one carried him out, but whenever he got close enough to a human, he would leap up and clamp onto bare skin with his mouth.

Bill, flat on his back under the truck as he replaced the muffler, endured neck nuzzling for a while, but it got in the way of seeing what he was doing. Mister B. was sitting astraddle his chest, and atop some of the tools, too. So he pushed Mister B. away. I was watching from outside, where I was free to go after tools, and saw Mister B. back off, then come at Bill's face with pointy jaws wide open, teeth held rigid and lips curling, screeching like a banshee. Small though he was, his exhibition was almost scary.

Bill snapped his wrist at Mister B.'s jaw in a back-sweeping motion, and received a hanging-on bite. A tap on the muzzle with Bill's other hand brought more of the same. There was no way to "explain" to Mister B. calmly: "Look, I'm busy and you're in the way. Wait awhile and I'll tolerate you—but not right now."

"Right Now!" Mister B. screeched in return. "Or I'll bite your eyes out." He looked as though that was what he intended, but he was so nearsighted that I doubt he knew what his jaws were pointing at—he knew only that he had been dislodged and, so, rejected. When he finally turned

away and walked down the length of the prone mechanic and onto the grass, he muttered dire imprecations in bear language, bawling, screeching, and snuffling all at once, like a child who has been paddled for something he does not believe he was doing "wrong." Then he sensed my presence and hopped up onto my knees for a nuzzling session at my underchin. But even while doing that, he snorted and bellowed between mmm-m-mum's.

Such temper tantrums occurred several times daily for about two months. Then he quieted or matured and it happened less frequently and finally, at five or six months, almost not at all. Although he always continued to nuzzle, even when getting on toward a hundred pounds and a year of age, he came, finally, to understand that it was not a rejecting thing to separate his muttering mouth from his human host, and then he could be dislodged without difficulty. But as an urchin he had an infinite capacity for rage. "He seems to have a pressure on the brain," Bill said, but to me it seemed more like a pressure on the heart, for it stemmed from needing acceptance.

Some nights he went to sleep quietly enough, on a lap or in the curve of a human arm, and then could be transferred to his sweater pile in the workroom. But early in the morning he would be up and about; and if I wanted to try for a few luxurious last winks, I would have to suffer for them while Mister B. ran up and down my back, under the covers. His claws dug in with more than a tickle. I kept the covers tightly around my neck, preferring back scratches to the hunger-bites he was capable of giving my nose and eyebrows.

It reminded me of the times when as a child of three to five I had dived into my father's bed early in the morning.

He had told me stories of the bears he and his brothers and sisters had encountered while berrying and going to school across Lewis River from their Clark County homestead in the early 1900s. But those had been bears for viewing, and retreating-from or pursuing. This one, in my own bed, was for running up and down the spinal column with twenty scratchy claws.

I rose earlier after Mister B. joined the household. He was not coddled but simply treated as an inhabitant of the house-cave, having equal rights, but not those of visiting royalty. The treatment he received was impartial.

The trilliums, as usual, made their three-petaled white flames in the woods under the tall trees (laying their striations of too much perfection on the heart), scintilla of pure white, yellow-pollened, in the green country. In those days we were doing the final readying of the sawmill site, waiting for the mill to be moved in; and I was splitting cedar posts, until there was a trio of piles, 150 apiece, in the front areaway. As we returned from the woods, we would be likely to hear the screeching of Mister B. His voice carried through the insulated walls of the house and across the field.

Both companionship and food he hungered for. The food I could provide, but constant companionship was not possible, at least not until he gathered a modicum of strength, for his two nights in the woods, motherless and chilled, had nearly sapped his last energy, which had been down to a low ebb as it was.

Food, then, came first. He acted the glutton, like Dr. Samuel Johnson, as if he had never had enough to eat in infanthood, and could never catch up. As a matter of fact, he *had been* short-rationed. His mother's activity had used up some of the body strength that might otherwise have gone into making milk. Her nervousness, due to the logging activity, had probably also dried up the founts of his youth. Now there was a plethora of fresh cow's milk, and he took to it as any small wild animal will, even mice and little spotted skunks.

At first he was fed in a crockery dish like those used for rabbits. The instant the bowl was filled it became "mine, all mine!" He clung to a human leg and wailed while the dish was filled with milk, oatmeal mush, and peaches. Then the dish had to be set down quickly and the human hand retracted. With yowls and growls he guarded it as if with his very life while he gobbled it. He buried his muzzle in it, up to the eyes. The eyes kept looking balefully out over the rim of the bowl, and he made bubbling yowls into the food even while devouring it. The house kittens fell back, abashed. His thick forearms went around the bowl and he clutched it like a life preserver in heavy seas. He embraced the bowl fiercely, taking it to his heart while introducing its contents to his taut, round belly. Almost at once he had ceased to need to be fed with a spoon, being unable, in his eternally "starving" condition, to get food quickly enough that way. He may have taken it too fast, and some of his post-eating yowls may have been of stomach-ache, but he never regurgitated or otherwise showed signs (such as scours, in calves) of radical indigestion.

When he grew larger and had to be fed in a bread-baking pan, he became a dog in the manger. He would sprawl out full length in the shallow pan full of milk, his underfur all in it, his forearms clutching the far corner outside, and his nose just at milk-level inside, his mouth buried. He was like a boat moving forward in the pan: fixed, yet "full speed ahead" (one could see it on the "engine-room telegraph" of his one-way mind).

Sometimes he would put one paw into the pan and nurse over the top side of it, as if the paw were an improvised nipple. When the pan was empty, he would lick his paws and arms, to get the last.

The domestic animals did not then, or ever, question his authority with *his* eating bowl. With some wild animals they had not been so respectful. One of the house kittens had once made the mistake of spitting at a pet mink who was lurking under a kitchen cabinet near the milk bowl. Then the cat had turned her back to drink. In a moment she was whirling over the kitchen tile, all four feet in the air and screeching like a fiend, tethered by her tail, which the mink held firmly between her own sharp front teeth. I frightened the mink off, releasing the cat, but she was forever afterward without a tip to her once long, glossy tail.

Mister B.'s breakfast had to be ready when his appetite commanded, and if the oatmeal were overlong in cooking, he would climb the cook's leg, clawing and wailing.

He was a ludicrous tyrant, foreshortened all over, from bare-rimmed eyes to a tail that was just a few thickened hairs, like a gnawed-off pencil. His face had, in those early days, the only resemblance to a grizzly's physiognomy that it would have—a slight dip just above the muzzle. On grizzlies the dip is higher up, making them dish-faced.

But there was nothing humorous about his attitude toward food. With familiar, household items such as mush and honey, applesauce and canned peaches, milk and dairy feed (we did not give him dog food because of the meat content, not wishing him to get a taste for meat or its flavor) he was a hog.

One day while we were out, he climbed to inspect the narcissus bulbs in a drainboard dish garden, and gobbled them all at one sitting. This pleased me, because I never was one for growing plants indoors, and when they bloomed, as they sometimes did, albeit about three months behind schedule, they were always lopsided, scrawny, with greens that reached practically to the ceiling, hiding the anemic off-white blossoms. There's one batch I won't have to suffer for, I thought.

But with some foods he could act like a connoisseur. When the first roses bloomed and I put some before him in the middle of the lawn, he lay out belly-flat and delicately tongued the inside surfaces of the petals, seeming to get as much joy out of the licking sensation as the taste. Then he chewed them, meditatively, and swallowed.

When he began going to the woods with us, he gummed daintily at cedar and hemlock twigs, as he had in the cave. Then he climbed to lick and chew the first vine-maple buds. When the vine-maple leaves came on, he mumbled them in his mouth, sometimes swallowing, sometimes spitting them out. In late May I saw him take the rounded, un-folded frond-end of a brake fern in the woods road into his mouth and, apparently, swallow. The same day, like any in-fant, he ate sandy soil from a damp declivity in the road.

In May, too, the six-petaled starflowers bloomed above mossy banks in the woods. From childhood I recalled their tuber, like a tiny, white-skinned potato, at the base of their straight stem, and the hairlike rootlets extending from it. Mister B. did not discover these roots, although had I taken the time to show them to him, I think he might have rel-ished them. Being fed so well above ground, he did not commence, early in life, to dig for bulbs, brake-fern roots, or the underground hiding places of mice, as adult bears were doing even while snow still covered the ground (the ground was a "map" of their passing in some places).

I should have showed him the starflower bulbs, simply "for his own good." I am glad that these are the kinds of things to recall from my own childhood: starflowers; frogs in the pond the cool spring made in the woods; cows and pumpkins; snails and a geode. The only halfway frightening thing was the darkness of the far woods when I was sent out at dusk to latch the chicken-house door. But what if I had approached life through the nightmare world of taverns and pinball machines, violence and outrageous conflict at home? Then I should not have as my first impressions these simple things: frogs; snails in their shells; a geode and starflowers. I should not feel "at home" on earth, but only outraged at having to live here.

About his first ants Mister B. was likewise delicate. We were splitting grape stakes by the millsite one May afternoon, and opened a log whose hollow center hosted a colony of ants. The cub licked out with his long, lolling tongue and got one. He tasted it, puzzled. Then another. It bit him. Then he lay on the opened-out log and rolled in ants, head back and at a lower elevation than the rest of him. He moved to the hillside and lay on his back, looking down and pawing the small, crawling things from his stomach hair. He seemed to find them amusing small fellow creatures, but he did not begin to eat them until several more months had passed.

In June I tried to show him how to catch grasshoppers. These, I knew, were a source of food, for my friends Lois and Herb Crisler had some movie footage of Olympia National Park bears shooing grasshoppers into a mountain stream, then scooping them up as the insects lay, trapped, on the water's surface. I tried him on large ant eggs, too; but he did not take to them nearly as immediately as he did to the first of spring's berries.

Instead of eating ants, he "rolled" in them. Perhaps the sharp formic-acid scent which they give off when disturbed intrigued him, or perhaps it was the tickling sensation as they crawled through his fur. Later, he learned to go after ants and grubs for food; he had certain favorite logs and stumps for them. I do not know what quantity he ate; well-fed as he always was at home, he probably had them only for appetizers, or mild exercise, in a desultory sort of way.

Even with fruit he could be a connoisseur. When the crab-apple tree, which had bumper crops on alternate years, labored and brought forth a single apple, Mister B. inspected it tenderly day after day for nearly two weeks before he finally brought it to earth.

His household gluttony finally got him barred from the house, except when humans were also inside. We returned from the woods one noon to find that he had climbed to the kitchen counters and, in passing, had kicked or clawed one of the controls of the built-in range. A burner was on "Low" and an oatmeal box which he had tipped over had rolled onto the burner and was charred along its lip. Little "Smokey the Bear" might have gone up in smoke had he turned the range to "High," and that was not what we had in mind for him, or for the household.

Male bears are called "boars" and females "sows." Mister B.'s attitude toward food made the labels meaningful: for the most part, his appetites and digestive capacities were most hoglike. And also humanlike. And while he did not bring to food the same kind of ceremonious respect the Indians do, one could see how their feeling of closeness to bears had grown from their observation that our two species eat the same foods.

V *Meeting Strangers*

In the household Mister B. lived with affection but without undue attention. When a visitor lavished upon him unaccustomed floods of fondness, he went berserk. It threw his whole emotional complex out of direct drive and into some runaway between-gears which only a solid swat could repair.

One evening a seagoing friend of Bill's and his wife came to Tiger Mountain. As we sat in the front room, the lady—a gentle and affectionate person—took Mister B. on her lap. For several hours she cuddled and crooned to him. While we discussed ships and cargoes, she and Mister B. were in a world of their own, one softly lamplit with mother-child affection. The cub responded with a lassitude and gentleness quite unlike his usual roughhouse self. I did not realize until after the visitors had departed that he had, in the space of a few hours, become "rotten spoiled."

I stayed up to read. Normally, Mister B. would have balled up on my lap to read the dreams of cubland slumber, peacefully, without asking to be fondled or talked to. But this evening he twitched and clambered all over me, sharp-clawed. He sat on my book and, when removed, came back to nip and complain. He made it clear that *he*, now, was the center of the universe; since I was slow to comprehend that, he would show me.

My system required a margin of peacefulness around each day: early morning and late evening, at least, were mine. His insistence upon tormenting me out of "my" final moments of tranquillity finally hit me where I lived. Reaching for a magazine, I rolled it and landed a swat across the top of his head.

At that, Mister B. "lost his head." Screaming horribly, he zigzagged around the room, burrowing his head into the rug, sliding headlong into an angle of the far wall, holding his forepaws over his head and face. He screamed! It was not a lonesome wail, a "feed-me" whine, or a "let-me-out-of-here" yammer. Those could be loud enough to be heard across the field, but this was catastrophic!

I was used to his small violences, but this one scared me. Could that swat have been enough to cause concussion? I had thought him to have a skull as solid as rock, but perhaps it was actually as tender as a baby's. Cornering him in one of his wild gyrations, I felt his head for lumps (none) and looked at the corners of his eyes where a thin rind of white showed: they were bloodshot!

But all that I could do was to let him "yelp it off." Finally he simmered down to occasional convulsive shudders and minor cries. He did not come to me again but, instead of going into the workroom to sleep, slouched into my room and up onto the bed. I found him there when I retired. He was in a deep, screamed-out sleep, limber as an old rug, and I could feel his small bulk against my back all night.

In the morning he was "fresh as a daisy," the white, wild daisies, golden-centered, in the high front field after rain. As fresh and bitey-scratchy as usual. But the tiny whites at the corners of his eyes were still red-webbed.

After that, I never swatted him anywhere but on the rump or, lightly, with the back of a hand, on the nose. I also discouraged undue attention on the part of visitors. When he was treated offhandedly, merely as one member of the household and not a visiting dauphin, he remained well behaved, for a bear. He could sit on laps while reading progressed, but without being fondled; he could get into bed, but without being cuddled; he could go up and down the halls, into the kitchen and bathroom, but without undue comment on the fact.

Unaccustomed attention can make an emotional mess of a bear (or any small animal), and this is what has happened to many of our national park bears, especially when spasms of attention are interspersed with spaces of inattention. The poor creature doesn't know whether he's the crown prince of the forest, or the garbage collector; no wonder he throws tantrums.

Another time two couples, each with an infant a few weeks old, came calling. Upon spotting Mister B., the mothers deposited their human burdens down upon the davenport and took turns holding B. while the babies yowled.

When they left, one told me: "Any time you want to come down and baby-sit, I'll come up and bear-sit."

(I would recommend bear cubs, rather than cats, for motherly women, although—and here's a rub—they may have to take them to bear-cub psychiatrists if they insist upon lavishing too much love on them.)

Not all visitors felt the same sort of affection for Mister B. A forester of the Conservation Department, who called several times annually to inspect our tree crop, studied the cub, bright-eyed. "I know a woman who would sure like to have that bear," he said.

I thought that he meant someone living in the mountains, farther away from roads and human habitations, who would rear Mister B. in a safer locale. I was tempted, for Mister B.'s sake. "Who is she?"

"She has a tree farm," he explained. "School children go there on tours, to study trees and nature. She has paths all through the woods. And along the paths, at different points, she has placed stuffed animals."

Mister B. clopped his claws into my leg and climbed on up, clutching fiercely. "I much prefer being an outdoor exhibit right here," his manner said.

Human children had a definite affection or jealousy for the small bear, depending upon their own special "personality needs." Of two brothers who vacationed on the ranch, the younger, "outgoing" one enjoyed and was amazed by Mister B., and the cub climbed the crisscrossed piles of fence posts, or went along with him to the barn and creek. The elder, completely self-centered boy, who needed all attention for himself, carefully pretended that Mister B. did not exist; the cub acted similarly toward him.

The four children of a young neighboring couple were much in the house, since they passed it daily to catch the school bus. One day I asked that they refrain from ever feeding Mister B. meat, because I did not want him to develop a taste for it.

About half an hour later the younger girl was slipping him a lunchmeat slice out of her sandwich, undoubtedly hoping that he would thereby and forthwith be transformed into a ravening fiend who would immediately have to be

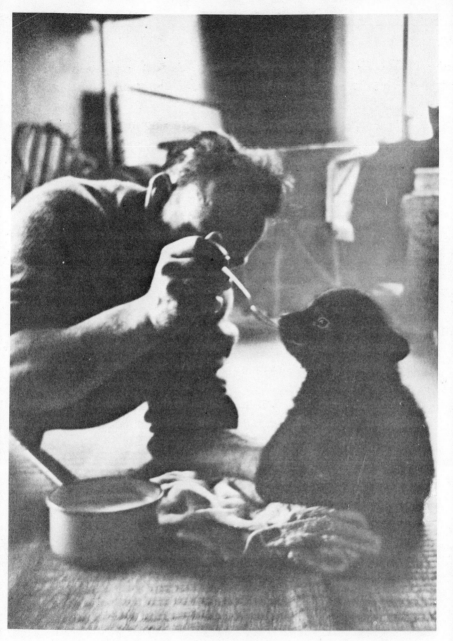

[1] *The author feeding Mister B. just after he was brought home.*
PHOTO BY ELLEN P. BEATY

[2] *The very young Mister B., all claws and bare-rimmed eyes.*

[3] *Bear in a basket.*   PHOTO BY ELLEN P. BEATY

[4] *His favorite bed warmer, next to humans, was Stella. Before they slept, he would nuzzle her silky ears or round little belly.*

[5] *Mister B. making friends during his first week at the ranch.*

[6] *"What big feet...." Mister B. at six months walking home after a swim in the creek.*

disposed of. For she was at an age or of a disposition which could not bear to share the limelight.

The neighbor at the little house across the driveway did not like Mister B., but on a different level. She said that I was "too permissive" with him, indicating, by her opinion, that she recognized his basically "human" personality. (As a matter of fact, while I recognized his need for independence, I was *not* permissive; "socially unacceptable" actions earned him a swat, and he learned the rules as readily as any normally intelligent little human does.)

One day she called me on the phone: "Come and get your bear out of my house. He's in the bathroom eating soap."

Just as I reached her screen door, another neighbor drove in from the main road. "Just came by to let you know that your cows are out on the road," he said.

"I'll be up there to get them in a few minutes," I told him. From within the house I could hear the small sounds of Mister B. at work. Still, I had to stand there till the neighbor small-talked a little more and drove away; I couldn't very well tell him: "Pardon me while I get a bear out of the bathroom."

I knocked and went in to get Mister B., who was on the kitchen table by now. I had him by the back when the neighbor lady reached to lift his foot out of the ashtray. That did it, for him, for he would take a reprimand from me, but not from her. Quick as a cat, he darted his head around and bit her hand, then turtle-necked back into my grasp, moaning, pretending great rage, but actually not knowing what punishment to expect next.

The neighbor's reaction surprised me. "He acts without

thinking," she said mildly, and gave a brief psychological dissertation on why Mister B. was as he was.

She could "explain" him but she never particularly liked him. The feeling was mutual. Mister B. developed weird little ways of getting back and of showing disdain—from galloping over her roof while she was trying to sleep to lunging flat-pawed against her picture windows or foot-punching the top of her ancient Packard convertible. He did these, and other devious tricks, with studied maliciousness, she thought. She may have been right, for he was sensitive to rejection or criticism, and even to the mood in which it was presented.

Mister B. and my brother were likewise mutually unsympathetic. "He's a *real* delinquent type," Paul said. "We had company in the house and he went from one to the other of their five fat little kids, testing for the one that was the juiciest to nuzzle on. I finally had to put him outside. He climbed a little tree to just out of reach and sat there, snarling and shooting me evil looks that said more than the foulest curses."

But he could, also, perform admirably for persons who were properly appreciative. When my cousin shot movies of him climbing trees, crossing the creek, walking, ambling, trotting, and running in the woods, he realized that he was the focus of attention. Long after the film had run out, he kept on performing. Years before, we had placed a twenty-foot, six-by-eight-inch timber crossways between two maple trees growing on a small shelf of a field above the creek canyon. Now, for the first time so far as I know, Mister B. climbed to the timber, as to a stage, and strutted upon it.

"Look," my uncle said, "he's putting on an act for us."

That "look" was all Mister B. needed; he went into perfect spasms of action.

He was always conscious of his ability to create interest, and sometimes he took stage center when I preferred that he would not. He liked to follow Nameless, and since she had a habit of waiting for me at the main-road gate all day long when I was on the mail route, Mister B. was near the road, too, where I did not want him to be.

One day when I got home in midafternoon, Nameless was waiting but the cub was nowhere in sight. A few minutes later, from the yard, I heard a car squeal to a stop out on the road. I walked out to discover a young couple from down the valley looking up into the top of a forty-foot fir tree. There, like a black moon in the treetop, sat Mister B.

"We've lived around here for ten years and have never seen a bear," the young man told me.

His attitude reflected the sense of wonder of most persons who happened to see him, and their almost universal tendency to leave him alone. They enjoyed simply viewing him, alive and free. Their common thought, sometimes expressed, was: "Anyone who would shoot one of those would have to be some kind of cretin who would murder his own grandmother if she had a good hide."

When these viewers had driven on, I called Mister B., in case a less considerate type might see him. He came down, limb by limb, in a desultory "I'll-take-my-own-sweet-time-Daddy-o" manner fit to burst my blood vessels. He was like a child just beyond reach in a mud puddle and reluctant to leave. "I'm waiting to impress another audience," his manner said.

He waited until he got within reaching distance of the ground and, when I came to lift him out, dashed up a few limbs. He looked down and around, independently, almost nastily, sensing my wish to get him out of there and not wanting to come—partly, perhaps, for the very reason that he knew it was what I wanted, so that it became, in his present mood, something that he wanted *not*. For, in all ways, he was almost human. But when I turned and went back toward the house, he came down fast enough and followed me. "Human" to the end.

From that time on, I took the mail route in an agony until time to speed home and see that Mister B. was still there. Nameless would be, I knew; but who might have scooped up the tiny cub and made off with him? In my dreams I saw him stuffed.

Mother bears, at least those still living outside national-park boundaries, and so still "fit" mothers, know how to keep their cubs off the highways. The former carrier of Route 1, out of Issaquah, described the actions of such a mother.

"I was on the old road between Fall City and Preston, about where it goes under that high trestle," he said. "There was a bear cub right in the middle of the highway, just fooling along, like a stupid kid. The mother came charging out from the side of the highway, took her paw and whopped that cub. Man, it was like a gigantic drop-kick! She landed him clear up in the front yard of one of the few houses along there!"

That mother must have felt the anxiety I had when the cub was on the road. I never did have the good sense to drop-kick Mister B. off to one side, however, partly because I didn't have a mother bear's weight advantage.

My most poignant picture of Mister B. and society remains that of his meeting with the two human mothers who had dropped their own infants to cuddle him. One of the mothers kept crooning to the bearling: "Oh, isn't he just precious!"

Mister B. gave me a precocious "wink" such as any petted child will give its parent under like circumstances: a look self-consciously angelic yet with a fiendish gleam in it. *He* knew just about how "precious" he *really* was—and so did I.

VI *Spring Night on the Mountain*

At the same time that I responded to being "needed," Mister B.'s close attachment to human beings bothered me. I had seen the outcome of divided loyalties in a young human; he had been pulled and tugged so many ways that, eventually, he could not be truly loyal to anyone on earth, not even to himself. It was a tragedy I did not have in mind for Mister B.

"Now he is strong and fat: he can stand a day or so in the woods," I told Bill. "He should get back with his mother now, if there is any chance for it."

Bill agreed. First, then, we scouted the mountain area for the cub's family. Our logging roads ran back to the rear of the property; beyond that, the land was wild for four miles in one direction, seven miles in another. Some of the logged-off land had grown up to a temperate-climate jungle of deciduous trees; in patches the evergreens were slowly coming back; on some of the upper ridges the soil had washed away after logging, leaving land that was unfit for anything but fern, salal, Oregon grape, and scrub vine maple; other ridges had never been logged.

54

The mother bear had many square miles in which to choose her relocation, but we felt that she had probably not gone far and that she had probably stayed fairly close to a stream. There was an upland swamp, lush with skunk cabbage, grass, and wild berries, at the far corner of our land, and we believed that she might be there—if it were not already the territory of another bear. We began where we had last seen the other cub and had heard the mother coming back through the hillside brush, and tried to trace her.

It had been several years since I had had reason, or excuse, or a margin of free time in which to ramble over the mountainside. Now, I saw it freshly. Looking at the Pacific Northwest mountains, one sees a gray-green land, overcast with cloud. It does not, immediately, strike joy to the spirit, as when, awakening on shipboard in the harbor of Santos, Brazil, one is bombarded with vivid color: bright sea, *blue* sky, green jungle shot through with the blue or orange tiles of habitations which hit the retina like buckshot.

Color pierces the gray-green here in the Northwest, but the eye must go out to meet it halfway. In April one must stoop to the pink of native orchids, the coralroot. The rattlesnake plantains were in bloom, each bloom a perfect miniature orchid, but tiny—their stalks rising up and their tongues turned groundward, so that one must bend and twist and turn the stems to see them. They do not flaunt flamboyantly, as in the jungle, from overhead tree trunks and mossy limbs; they are not flags hung out—they are small flames turned downward. They are symbolic of all color in the rainy, Western land.

The broad-leaved maples hang down their racemes of yellow-green. A small wind sizzles the bronzy first leaves of the poplar trees. Wild currants dangle their clusters of crimson or pink bloom (depending upon the amount of sunlight they get) close above the ground, and the first hummingbirds hover before them. But it is all color that must be looked for; it does not bombard the eye.

As we followed up the mostly green jungles of brush that had taken the ravines following logging, the small, muted colors came alive to me again. Even the rocks and boulders in the creeks displayed a spectrum, if one looked closely enough: black, green, and blue, jasper-red with veinings of white quartz, the white of pure quartz, the black-flecked white of granite, the amber or gray-opal of agate.

We saw, too, what we were looking for: bear signs. Grass had been grazed in the upland swamp. In one place skunk cabbages had been uprooted and the glistering-white roots, like those of leeks, were exposed. The tender growth of ferns had been crushed by a heavy animal's passing. Some of the cedar and alder trees bore on their bark the claw marks of climbing.

Where these vertical trails were most pronounced, along the bank of a ravine northeast of the cave about a quarter of a mile, was a likely place, we decided, for Mister B. to contact his family.

After dusk the following evening we put the cub into a large metal box and loaded him on the back of the pickup. He was well fortified with a last supper of milk and canned peaches. Over his muted wails and desperate clawings of protest Bill drove to the far end of one of our roads and turned around. He opened the box and carried Mister B. to the area where climbing-marks indicated his mother must be. Then Bill gave him the slip, returned to the truck, and drove home.

For two days, then, we stayed out of the woods. On the

evening of the second day, we walked mountainward, to see if the experiment had succeeded. The five dogs went along. We had let them come, thinking that they would follow in silence, but as soon as we were on the mountain the female beagle began baying her foolish head off, running overlapping circles on cold scent-trails.

Shortly after she "opened up," we heard Mister B. squalling an answer from the hillside beyond the spot where Bill had left him.

I caught the beagle and carried her home, calling the other dogs to follow; in case the mother bear was near, I did not want them to upset her. Bill went on up toward Mister B.'s continuous, high-pitched wailing.

After dark he returned with the cub in his arms. "He was up a little fir tree, crying his eyes out. It was pitiful," Bill said.

When the cub had gorged himself, he climbed into one of the chairs and fell asleep in a tight ball. His fur rippled and twitched with almost visible bad dreams.

He was no closer to being reunited with his family than he had been at the moment his mother had deserted him in the woods near the den. We felt that she had certainly been within hearing distance of him on the mountainside the past two days, but still did not want him. At first she had rejected him because (a) he could not keep up or (b) he was, with the other cub or cubs, taking too much of her milk or (c) a combination of these plus the fact that she may have been fearful of returning past human smells and the sounds of human woods-work to get him and lead him onward. Having once rejected him, she did not, apparently, wish to re-accept him, although she certainly could have told, from his voice, that he was hers.

"There is only one thing to do," I said, being as bear-headed, myself, as Mister B. and his mother combined, "feed him up and try again."

So, we did. He was starved: first, for food; and, second, for affection. In a week, when he had regained his plumpness and independence, we popped him into the metal box and Bill made the mountain run again.

This time I could better envision his night upon the mountain. He would climb a small fir tree and wail himself to sleep. Toward midnight he would probably be wakened by the one-trill call of a white-crowned sparrow waking, briefly, in the top of a nearby tree. The midnight train would make its mournful whoo-whooo at the Landsburg Crossing. He would drowse again, but undoubtedly not get comfortable enough to really sleep.

Toward morning the rain began. It came in a downpour. Little birds were drowning in their nests. Broad-leaved trees, burdened by the wet, turned down their boughs. Through a lull in the downpour Mister B. might hear the roosters down at the ranch yard calling from tree to tree across the fields and from the barns, challenging dawn and one another. Smells, some strange and some familiar, would drift up to him before rain dampened them again.

Then, as the rain eased and the sky lightened, so that he probably felt lighter in spirit himself, he would back down the tree and fumble forward down the mountain toward home. He would walk with legs bowed, trying to escape the wet. Rain, held by low leaves, would fall upon him when he brushed the bushes, like upside-down umbrellas unloading. I could see him looking, as he often had, like two bow-legged cowboys walking tandem, or like a "horse" in a Boy Scout circus, which is made up of two men inside a "hide."

As he walked along and came opposite a small swamp, the frogs would cease their chorus and then begin again after he had passed. The sky, which he could feel but could not see, "lifted" as he moved downward; one could suppose he had a feeling of lightheadedness, almost giddiness, that goes with walking in such light, so that he would lift his fore-paws higher than usual, as if he were walking up a stair at each forward step.

The leaves of the small poplar trees were all in motion, like a symphony of notes, turning and twisting upon their stems. And as the day came fully light, a horde of small birds fairly burst their throats with song.

Mister B. pushed on in the direction where, he knew, home lay.

For that time, when we were at the sawmill site the following day, Mister B. came down from the mountainside himself. A pygmy, dwarfed further by the trees on either side, he came whuffling and snuffling down the woods road, moaning low to himself, following some faint scent of the truck tires, or perhaps just feeling his way along the worn creases of the ruts. The ruts were slight because, being over rock, they were almost imperceptible to the eye, although they may have been freeways to his still tender pads.

What a pitiable dwarf he was, and the obvious human reaction was to lean down, scoop him up, and to enfold him in that comfort from which he had been, overnight, banished.

We tried the experiment one more time, and this third time Mister B. got all the way home by himself. He was taken to the mountain one evening. At 2:30 in the morning he was scratching and clawing on the wall outside the bedroom window, whining for his ration of peaches. When I brought him in, his fur was soaking wet; he had fallen in the big creek on his way over.

That put a period to it; Mister B. was home to stay!

There might still, I thought, be one halfway-house compromise: Mister B. might mature to the point where he could sleep at the cave by himself and come to the house to be fed and to romp. Later, he might come to prefer the woods altogether.

So we began taking him to the cave, feeding and leaving him there. One of the first times it almost worked, in a sense, until my own concern put an end to it. We took him to the cave one near-dusk and left him there with a pound coffee can full of peaches and warm milk.

The following day a pack of beagles brayed up and down the woods near where he was. Would they chase him off, or would a solitary German shepherd, deserted and gone "wild" enough to kill and devour some of our hens with chicks, capture him? We went to the cave entrance, called, stood, and listened. No more bear-singing this season.

"He's gone!"

We were just turning away when out he came, rubbing sleep from his eyes and "grumpy as a bear with a sore head." Nasty-mad, he did not offer to climb a leg or beg to be picked up. But by the time he had followed us home, he had worked himself out of the mood, as any child-thing will after a nap: they don't want to *begin* it; they don't want to *end* it.

Other times, thereafter, we would take him to the cave and feed him. But he would not be left. He would gobble the food and, even before we were out of the woods, he would emerge by another trail ahead of us on the road. The first time out he may have followed Nameless; after that he beat her out, too, or came out beside her, twirling half-erect to cuff her flanks as they ran.

When there was no further question of reuniting Mister B. with his wild family, I was almost as relieved as I would have been had the reuniting "taken." For Mister B. accepted me completely. There was never any need to "work" at try-ing to get along with him. That was the rarest of his beau-ties. All that I needs must be, in order to please him, was body-warm and food-providing. My grouchiness he could easily endure, having suffered worse from his mother and more than matching me, sometimes, with his own. He did not notice if a button was missing or if shaving had been delayed a day. Bad breath did not convulse him and he did not hint that what one *really* needed was a good, roll-spread-spray-and-glue-on deodorant.

He always accepted me as I *was*, truly for better and for worse. For this reason, in part at least, I suppose, I never had a mean thought for him, and almost always had to smile when I saw him close-up or from afar, even when he was being ornery. I had worried (and would, in future) when he was out of sight for long periods. But he, himself, never disgusted me. There was a happy toleration on both sides; and I think that if such a feeling were possible between human beings, at home and in the larger human family of the earth, creative competition would take the place of wasteful conflict.

Sophisticated persons point to the impossibility of such a course in "our complex society." A "complex" is as complex as we make it. A man cannot very well meet *himself* in a "meeting." If individual man could learn to tolerate himself, and then his household and his wider range of associates, he might in time come to be capable of tolerating the family of man. Possibly it is too "simple" a thing to ask of man. Too simple and too dull. We customarily think of our daily lives as being so prosaic that a dash of "neighbor trouble," at home or abroad, looks like adventure. "Let's get some action!" the young men say.

Mister B. spiced up the pattern of ranch life. Although he was not universally admired, I never had any temptation to think of him, as one often does of the persons closest to one, as a mortal enemy. He was a mortal friend—not a "subject," but an equal—always with his own personality, and that not a belittling, but rather, a growthy one. He expected great things of life. Even the beast in him brought out the best in me.

I am not sure of how well this acceptance on his part would have lasted once he reached adulthood. But I believe that, as has occurred with both male and female deer reared by humans, he would have gone forth to the mountains on early-summer mating treks and returned to visit the ranch and its inhabitants in other seasons.

The basis for such a relationship existed: it was an association totally without fear, on either side.

VII *He Rediscovered Nature to Me*

From visitors who pause and pass after hours or years, depending upon their needs or purposes, the householder learns many things. New thoughts may be planted in his mind's garden while the visitor helps him to dig potatoes. Companionship before the evening's firelit hearth may bring new understanding of the human heart. With some visitors a lifetime's stay would be too short; others make an hour seem like an eternity underground.

Mister B., from his first clutching grapple at my sleeve, had settled in for a long visit. I had been tentative about it myself, and had hinted broadly that he should return to the woods. Some visitors heed hints; some don't. It was just as well that he didn't; thanks to him, it became my spring for rediscovering a world that had lain dormant in the past few years, when my concerns were mainly for persons.

Nature was re-revealed through his senses, as he walked out upon this earth. He "saw" as through a glass, but not darkly. The world had a glowing freshness for him, and through him, for me.

63

Mister B.

He had that persistent curiosity which is common to all wild creatures, even insects. When the thin-winged, French-blue butterflies of April flew up and down as if attached by silken threads to a certain spot on the pasture track, he stood and watched their patterns against the sun, his forepaw half lifted. There were five of them in the same spot several days in succession, and he always paused. They hovered toward his back, "tasting" his fur.

Ears up, he attended upon frogs singing in the swamp beyond the bedroom window in mid-April. At night, or toward dawn, he would be drawn that way, like a fish on a leader, and I walked out with him to ease his going. When we got to a certain sound-boundary, they all ceased, their silence spreading back in a wave from the near edge of the swamp to the woods at the far side. Mister B. looked up and back at me, like a child asking youth's perpetual "why?" If we waited silently, minutes later, as on a cue, they all began again—simultaneously.

After we had made the trip out several times, I used to hear them from my bed: singing, ceasing. Sometimes their abrupt silence wakened me. Lying still, I did not know why. What had gone by them in the night? What swooping wing or velvet pad or crackle of brush or bending-down of grass? What dark passer in the otherwise secure, moat-and-mud-mellowed swamp? (And why did the heart have its answering pause, its cessation?)

He never pawed or tried to eat a frog; his mother had not had time to teach him that. He did contact garter snakes. Once, in the feed lot by the hay barn, I came upon him in his stand-and-stare of wonderment. Looking past him, I saw seven half-bantam chicks lined up, heads cocked, entranced to silence. They were a brood whose mother had left them early to rear themselves. They were looking at a morning-chilled garter snake with a red stripe.

"This enemy, our ancestor!" their stiff-kneed stances said.

Mister B. shouldered them aside to lay the flat of his paw upon the harmless reptile. He rubbed it, back and forth, without clutching. When it wriggled, he reared up and did a dance backward on his hind legs, then bent forward to paw it again.

There was a garter snake who lived along the road to the creek with whom he had a closer acquaintance. Because this snake was in the same location day after day, I learned that snakes may have their own territories as surely as birds have theirs. Whenever Mister B. met this particular snake, he went into his ritualistic dance of touch, back up, and touch again; the snake responded with mild loopings and unloopings; the tongues of both small animals were out as they tasted the mutual air. They reminded me of neighbors meeting on a city street or by a bus stop at the same time of the day, every day, and making the same ritualistic motions. They met, went into their "meeting dance," and parted. Friends? Well, contacts, at least. But if Mister B. could be a friend to me, then why not to a garter snake? If he could bring emotional reactions to meetings with and separations from me, and he visibly *could*, then why not dissimilar but definite reactions to meetings with the snake? Perhaps their meeting was a specific event in the snake's day, too.

One morning I turned over a small, loose cedar stump to carry it in to the fireplace. Under it a large snake coiled, napping, beside its castoff skin. Mister B. carried the skin on his paws, "showing" it to me. For the first time, I really looked at a snake's skin. I saw that he had crawled out of it head-first, for that was where the only split occurred.

Even the skin covering the eyes had been shed. The cicada's castoff skin, tougher, has a split down the back. The cicada *backs up* out of his skin; the snake *goes forward* out of his.

Would that the human spirit could thus shed its emotional traumas, I thought, as Mister B., begging for the skin back, took it and tongued it and delicately ripped it asunder with his front claws.

He was forever sniffing, tonguing, and touching things. Bowling down a woods road, he would suddenly stand upright and with one forepaw bend down a vine-maple limb and take the leaves into his mouth. Farther along, he would taste damp sand on the edge of a horse-hoof crater. When the wind blew fluff from the cottonwood trees, he examined it critically with tongue and paws. Wherever he went, his long, seemingly double-jointed tongue was apt to be out, as if he were tasting the air-borne scents. Some mornings a cloud would be moving across the front field a few feet above the ground, and he would stand on his hind legs to "taste" it.

On the morning of May 3 some tall dandelion stems already wore the halos of seed. Just a few mornings before there had been snow on the top of Tiger Mountain, but already the first yellow dandelions had gone to seed. Mister B. cuffed at the puffy balls, taking the seed umbrellas into his mouth; they stuck to his tongue like old-fashioned peanut butter.

Violet-green swallows were in the eaves and he reared up to look toward them. Following his gaze, I saw that they were like fish under water, schools of herring or candlefish, swirling and occasionally twirling their belly-sides upwards, flashing.

The fence rows were full of Scotch broom where we had

thrown seed several years ago. Daytimes, they were full of bird song, and Mister B. pointed his nose at them, listening. When he went out with me at midnight for the last check-up on the stock, the early May night was moon-misty. The perfume of the broom was on the air, the whole night scented, safe and beautiful. And the wild-cherry trees were blossoming, with a scent of spice—like the spice-cabinet aroma of Grandma Wolverton's kitchen, perfuming the whole ranch.

On the morning of May 20 a rusty blackbird male stood atop a back-yard fir tree spilling song, like diamonds cascading from a pouch onto black velvet. Up an adjoining maple tree went Mister B., to a level with the singer, and looked across at him.

One morning a few days later, as I went out to milk, Mister B. was at the top of the Dutch door leading into the garage, hanging on with his right forepaw and leaning far out to peer into the knothole opening to a swallow's nest. His object was not to eat the birds—he was not looking for food. Like his relative in the folk song, he merely "went over the mountain to see what he could see."

Trees were his special curiosity field. To Mister B. every tree in the forest sang a siren song: "Embrace Me." On the smooth-barked cedars he clopped his foreclaws in with a quick, wrist-bent gesture while his back feet dug in like a lineman using heel spikes. On trees too large to embrace, he moved up with forepaws above, instead of encircled, in jump movements of fold and unfold, like a furry black caterpillar with beady eyes and an upward-thrust golden nose.

He always descended backward, often self-consciously nonchalant, wearing a twig in his mouth like a toothpick. Once, on a rainbow-shaped vine maple, he slipped around until he was hanging underside like a three-toed sloth, and then fell crashing out on his back. The same day he broke off a dead limb high in a fir tree and came down, head over tail, through other limbs, crackling and whirling—about eighteen feet—whump! to the ground. But seconds later he was heeding another of the siren songs—as many as two hundred to an acre, not counting snags, stumps, and leaning logs. Every tree spelled adventure or, at least, amusement, to him. He disclosed to me life's infinite potential for variety, even in such mundane and everyday manifestations as trees.

The June woods played a rhapsody of sensation for him. He ambled into the pools and puddles of cool sunlight sifting through the trees. A fly bathing in light on a broad green leaf zizzzzzzed away, past his nose. A warty green-gray toad, with a yellow-green stripe from nostrils to anus, came breast-stroking across the woods road, slantwise, ahead of him. He lifted his head as two trees screeched together high overhead, consorting in a small treetop breeze. From high up, too, came the sound of swarming, as half a colony of wild honeybees left the home hive in a maple snag to make a crescent-shaped cluster about their new queen in a nearby hemlock tree.

The miner's lettuce was in bloom; Mister B. ate the pale blooms and the leaves, tentatively. He paused to consider the green woods slug sliding wetly upward along the slippery, sappy trunk of a cedar tree which porcupine, rabbit, or deer had debarked.

Along the ranch roads, wherever the rocky soil had been disturbed, a hallelujah chorus of foxglove seeds were tucked in and had germinated. Up in green floods came the ground-covering, dark-green plants whose broad leaves, when dried, make digitalis, a stimulant. Each plant shot up a single center spire, fishing-pole size. By late May, stalks of the more precocious plants were beginning to show bloom buds which, when open, would be like the small fingers of gloves—longer than thimbles. When pulled from the stalk, the stem-end is like a small reed stuck on the thimble, resembling somewhat the socket end of a TV picture tube. Children invariably wear them on their fingers, waggling their hands aloft in glee.

By the first week in June some were blooming, the white and off-white plants first, then the purple ones. Mister B. liked to stand up to the stalks of bloom, to bat or whop them with the flats of his forepaws. Paws on a stem, he might tip his head sideways and, with a small-boy grin, take some of the lower blooms into his mouth. The white or purple of the blooms above was reflected back in the dark irises of his eyes. The blooms' inner throats were flecked with dark spots, a small thing which he rediscovered to me.

In a fit of joy he might grab a five- or six-foot foxglove stem, as a rope climber would his rope, and pull it to ground. Sometimes where he had played in the foxglove fields it was as if a horseman had ridden through erratically.

One morning he was standing—nail-tips of one paw merely touching a stem, the other paw dangling at his side —looking up into a foxglove thimble. Following his gaze, I saw the rear, pollen-swollen legs of a bumblebee. The bee was buzzing in the thimble like a minor cyclone, shuddering the whole plant with his industry. As we watched, he backed out, tail-heavy, dropped backward, spread his wings, and took off, his bristle-haired body in dark contrast to the golden globs of pollen pantalooning each leg.

On the ranch roads Mister B. had eternal insect-meetings.

Mister B.

His growthiness made his contact with bugs more ludicrous as he braked to inspect a snail, a worm, or a shiny-black, hard-shelled millepede, which curled into a hard, round pinwheel when he ticked it with his nails.

He had an insatiable curiosity for nature's textures. When on June mornings cobwebs were like pygmies' parachutes laid out flat on the ground to dry, and the cobwebs that hung between strands of barbed wire on the fences were mist-beaded, he went at them delicately. And came along wearing a wisp of the sticky web across his nose.

He lifted his nose toward low-flying birds: wild, male canaries bobbing for pure, butter-yellow happiness on the pellucid air—making their zip-zip, yellow-and-black mark up and over the fences, the first line of alders, while their mates hovered eggs couched on feathers and cottonwood fluff. He paused, looking up, to where violet-green swallows fed their first brood on the top strand of the fence while, farther along, a pair of slower, brown-breasted barn swallows chittered—they having come north later and not even completed their mud-daub nests, let alone laid their first clutch.

His attentiveness discovered to me, again, that every bird has its own manner of flight, so that one could chart them, as on a graph—a job as exacting and perhaps as exciting as recording songs. In a sense it would be like writing music: the music of flight.

When the cows were kicking up blackbirds that followed them on the ground, or the horses clipping off daisy heads at a gallop, he bounded along, at a speed which sometimes outran caution, to see what was happening.

One morning when he was sitting at the end of the cow feeder, I took the last of a sack of mill run and dumped it all. Out rushed a mill-run-dusty little barn mouse. Mister

B.'s nose went up and down as if on a string attached to the mouse-perambulations along the feed trough. He looked, without pawing at it. He never did have the proclivity of many small humans to *grab* at whatever they see. Butterflies, mice, snails, bees, bugs—he would tick them with his nails or hold his paw *flat* at them, as if giving benediction. A woods-sharpened appetite would have provided him with a different set of reactions; but, as it was, he remained a wonderer, not a predator.

The gray mouse went out over the end of the trough and away. But later, Mister B. came in the field to a freshly-killed mouse, larger, and marked with deer-tan along the back and sides, silky-white below. He turned it over with his paw, discovering to me, again, that mice are as various in their markings as different breeds of cattle. This one was fit to be a fairy queen's sables.

Eternally, he "showed" me: the changeable blue of Western bluebirds' feathers, depending upon the light; the pain-bright, black-and-white markings of little more than mouse-sized "Holstein" weasels, drawn by curiosity from under a slab pile, retracted underneath again by caution. Together, we watched a red squirrel moving her young, one at a time, to a new nest. She carried them in her mouth, each as large as two bumblebees stuck end to end.

Patience, in matters less important than food to him, more important than food to me, he taught me. I had never been one to wait patiently for my destiny to come up the road: I must go down the road after it. And yet—there are always the chores of the morning to be done, followed by the day's work and evening's chores, again. Does one carry the farm on one's back, as Thoreau said . . . or is it not also true that the farm gives to one the solidarity of being needed, and also a certain peace (streaked with impatience)? So, one decides. Or, more likely, it is decided *for* one—by his upbringing and whatever forms his individual creativity takes.

Still, it is most difficult to wait, especially when one feels that he should have arrived long ago but the conductor refuses to call the station. The human spirit, eternally restless, never quite gets "used" to that harness, those blinders; one walks through the day, brushing occasionally at the corners of his eyes, as if to say: "Let this cloud lift."

And this impatience was something that Mister B. sometimes had to live with, having to live with me, had to bear his own share of. For, often enough, I had had "too much" when he had not even started to get half enough of the day's life. When we went to the woods then, we started out at cross and irritating purposes.

But, eventually, he would straighten things out. He was my leveler: he brought me low. His innocence humbled me; his passion for the miracles strung out along the roads and trails then raised me up; and, before the afternoon was out, life was in tune again. It was not his patience, for he was eternally impatient, too (especially in matters of creature comfort), but his simple gratification with the simple miracles of life. He helped to teach me, over again, what I already knew, just as he rediscovered to me colors and faces of nature that I had seen before, long ago.

Even so, life itself, if one remains long enough at a fixed point, will, like the sea, eventually bring in to one whatever his heart desires.

[7] *Mister B. took to the car with a curious devotion. Here he tears at insulation under the hood to make a nest.*

[8] *His mechanical ability was surpassed only by his curiosity. Here he inspects the chain saw.*

[9] *Mister B. exploring the terrain by the creek.*

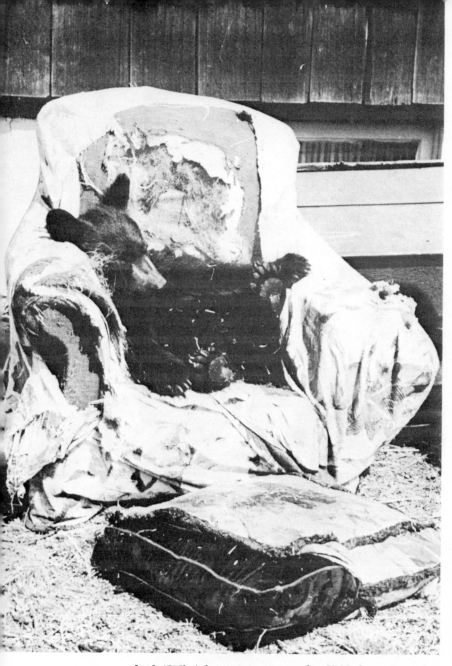

[10] *"Who's been sitting in my chair?" He knew it was his, and he un-upholstered it to his heart's content.*

[11] *Mister B. with a visitor. Toward humans he acted
and postured humanly.*

VIII *"Little Helper"*

Mister B. participated.

From the moment he could find his myopic way up the field and had strength in his legs to go, he helped with regular chores and with every other kind of work, as if the ranch were a youth program set up entirely on behalf of orphan bears.

He had the need of any healthy creature to play the game, not just to spectate and speculate. He was hard-cored with that inner necessity to keep a paw in which makes any life come *to life*. The eternal onlooker might as well be, himself, a specimen caught to dangle in a plastic charm, fixed for all times in a synthetic spell. Intriguing to look at, perhaps. But quite dead.

Social scientists caution: "You have let your feelings get involved," as if involvement were a childish mistake. Feelings are an aspect of love and have their own actions as surely as the body acts. From acted-out feelings comes man's greatest creativity, whether of art, craftmanship, or other life. I am glad for my feelings that they keep wild and free enough to *get* involved.

"It will bring you pain."

"As surely as it does, it shall also bring me moments of unalloyed joy," I reply, "the two being so close that in some hours I may not be able to say whether the tears I shed are of pain or bliss."

Mister B. knew all the violent pleasures and pains of involvement. After the space-capsule crampedness of his cave, the sudden appearances of the outside world must have been a sort of Saturn-landing to him: riotous with smell, zany with sound, uphumped with innumerable weird shapes, some of which broke into motion toward or away from him at his uncautious approach. (In some cases he did learn caution, but he never, I believe, feared.)

Persons, first, then horses, cows, and cars "moved" in his new universe. Bill and me he followed. Even that had its anxieties. Bill came in to report that the cub was apparently even more nearsighted than himself: "I was walking down the field from the barn with a pitchfork of hay. I stood still and he went right on past me, within a foot or two, going the wrong way. Talking to himself. I'm sure he didn't know that I was there."

I had reared a black-tailed buck deer from his first day to eighteen months. From the first moment he had recognized persons by scent; individuals he knew by their individual body odors, so that he would leave a resting-hiding place when a certain person passed, but continue hiding when other-smelling strangers went by. The cub had none of this scent-finesse. Of his senses, all dulled at first, hearing seemed the most acute.

Dogs he knew from knowing the yipping-barking harmlessness of Nameless and from discovering that Septic's snarl dissolved slowly, when snarled back at, like the Cheshire cat's grin. The inside information on horses and cows came harder.

One April morning when mist-furred earth held all her creatures as close to her as a mother opossum her young, Bill went out early to harness the horses. Mister B. rushed along, following with his high-shouldered gait, which made it always appear that he was about to lift himself into an erect, hind-legged run. He mounted the field, head and front end *up*, hind feet bicycling along behind. He reminded me of a nervous child learning to dog-paddle, his head held chin-tilted above the water.

As he followed the sound of footsteps he croaked throatily. "Where has my helper gone?" he maundered in lonesome tones. Before him loomed something similar to an overalls-leg but what was in fact the rear leg of the 1850-pound male member of the team of black Belgian work horses. The gelding, who had never been clutched by four sets of sharp claws in his venerable life, bucked. Mister B. dropped off, clutching a pawful of long, winter horsehair— only, in his nearsighted nervousness, to seek haven up a leg of the mare. Her reactions were even less receptive, and he narrowly escaped a stomping by a platter-sized hoof.

After that he left horse legs alone, but human limbs always remained fair climbing. And later on in the woods— Mister B.'s home ground—he was to do a job of horse-baiting which may have been tastily seasoned with memories of having been shaken off a hairy, mammoth-like leg or two.

April 1, the day the Western bluebirds returned that year, the Jersey cow had her calf in a grove of Douglas firs. Where she had been bovinely passive toward Mister B., she now became a horridly offensive mother creature. When the small black animal crossed the pasture, following one of his human co-workers, but often trailing at some distance, the cow rushed him. She did not dislike dogs, but apparently the cub stirred, in shadowy recesses of her mother "instincts," a passionate hate. She slavered, mooed, and pawed the thin scattering of spring grass with her front hoofs—right, then left. When she had worked herself into a proper frenzy, she lunged! Twice, in our sight, she caught up with him and tried to squish him into the ground with her hornless head. Bill rescued him from what he considered to be death's door the first time; I watched him squirm away and extricate himself the second. His screeching and fang-baring had no effect on the cow: she *bore down*, fairly standing on her head, with all her weight behind her and intending to grind him like a peppercorn under a pestle.

Mister B. developed a morning habit of making his own pre-chore round of the pasture. The other cows and heifers sniffed him and snorted, or silently followed along behind him, noses low, with their usual curiosity for an other-sized, other-perfumed creature. (How he smelled to them, I do not know; he had no odor that my civilization-dulled nostrils could detect.) But when the Jersey charged him, he bellowed in bear voice as belligerently as breath allowed, while rushing for the nearest stump (usually an untenable position) or post or manger of the calf shed. If he caught her immoderate attention in mid-field, he scuttled for the nearest fence post, not realizing, for some weeks, that he could effectively escape by merely skinning under the lowest strand of the barbed wire.

On this ranch the posts stand tall and thin-topped. Tall, for the rocky ground does not gracefully admit to digging deep postholes. Thin, for these are the culls that cannot be sold to other ranchers. Too lean to market, too sound to burn: I use them myself, just as, in former days, farmers denied their own families the cream: it was "too good" for them, and children who wished to test the mysteries of an ice-cream freezer or whose mothers needed a half-cup of cream for company's coffee had to slip into the milkhouse and filch it. Like conspirators they ladled out and used it. Eggs, too, were among the few products of a pioneer ranch that could be sold for flour-and-tax money. Chickens were pampered like golden geese and eggs were for careful cleaning and storing until they could be sold. One of the major tragedies of my father's early life (aside from the homestead buildings burning three times in forest fires) occurred when Grandmother's horse ran away with her, and the eggs she was carrying to sell at a logging camp were scrambled en route.

Thus, my own spindly fence posts. Mister B., hoisting himself to safety atop one, usually found the landing area to be slim. He screeched abuse down toward the Jersey and *"Save me"* toward the house. He was not cat-miserly with his voice. When he wanted rescue, or anything else, he *wanted* it, and *pronto*. One of my clearest mental pictures was like a sound-film. The picture was so acute that it did not seem needful of photographing; when I thought of doing so it was too late, like thinking of what one should have said to be scintillating on a TV interview already taped and canned for release next Sunday morning. In it the tiny cub was teetering atop a needle-pointed post, shooting screams for help, like flaming arrows, toward the house.

Innumerable times he was rescued and the cow chastised with shouts. To kick her otherwise kindly self would have been almost as disrespectful as doing likewise to one's mother, but she *did* have her savage side and Mister B. *did* bring it out; the fiend in them both emerged at their every meeting. When he was finally able to recognize at a distance which cow had the demon, he learned to keep their paths from crossing. He grew, eventually, to be calf-size himself, so that she had to tolerate him. Her tolerance was never synonymous with love.

She had always stood serenely in the open field to be milked, but her manner became skittery when Mister B. assumed his job as milker-helper. Torn between the lavish odor of fresh milk streaming into the bucket and memories of being brought to earth by the cow, he dawdled nervously beside and behind me as I milked. Sometimes he climbed my back and mumbled moistly at my neck. When he grew too large to be tolerated in that position, I would extend my left foot, providing an ankle as a pacifier for him to gnaw on.

He always preferred to be tactile in his helpfulness. The deer, who had come of age here, had likewise followed to the barns, post pile, and woods, but he had liked to stand alone at an individualized distance. Mister B. clung. When I had scythed the grass of the front field in the deer's company, he had stayed several times the scythe's arc away; Mister B. clung to my upper leg. When I had used the old crosscut saw, the deer had sometimes tongued the moving blade, from the opposite side of the log; Mister B. climbed my back and huddled there, monkey-like. Whatever the operation, he was not so much interested in it as in being physically close to the person doing it.

When in April we set up the portable sawmill at the lower edge of the side hill where we had been piling logs all winter, Mister B. "helped." His attitude said, plainly:

"You couldn't really do this right without me," and he stuck to us, literally, early and late.

When we began sawing, Bill rolled the logs onto the mill's movable carriage, and turned them with a peavey until they were squared off. The mill's owner stood on the carriage to one side of the thirty-six-inch blade and worked the levers which moved the mill back and forth, and made the settings which resulted in varying sizes of timbers and boards. I worked at the rollaway end, removing the slab sides to a waste pile, and taking the sawed lumber as it came out, piling it on the ground or on the flatbed truck which was backed up to one side of the rollaway's far end.

Mister B., of course, *had to* help. He would grapple my leg, just above the knee, for hours at a time. When his small-muskmelon-sized head bumped on the steel legs of the rollaway as I moved past them, guiding lumber coming from the saw, he would make complaining "ouch" wails every time he hit, and cling all the tighter, digging in with needly claws.

The price of passion: getting hit on the head every few minutes! He had an infinite capacity for punishment—not as a masochist, for he disliked the pain, but as payment for the affection he desired.

When his small weight turned to lead on my leg, I unbuckled him, leg by leg, like an octopus, and he ducked under the slapping pulleys running from motor to mill, and headed for Bill at the other end.

When we put him into the cab of the truck, for his own protection as well as our relief, he climbed to the window and hung backward down the slippery outside of the door. He could feel no toehold down the door's side. Wailing, he slid back and forth along the window ledge. Finally, he found that he could swing his left hind leg out and get at the lumber being loaded on the truck bed; by gyrating fiercely then, he could swing himself down and around, onto the load. Thence, he backed from the truck bed around and under to the top of a tire, scrabbled down the tire to the ground, and rushed to help again.

After that we rolled up the cab windows. Sometimes he would give up and sleep on the floor or truck seat. But if it was not nap time (and his system had a regular schedule, so that if it was *not* time, he would *not* nap), he sounded off to make Babel blush. Above the sound of the motor and the whirling saw blade with its furry blur as it ground through the tough-grained hemlock logs, we could hear his complainings.

When we left him there to go to lunch across the creek, we could sometimes hear his screeches of sociable protest clear across at the house. He had a voice that carried like that of a jackass at a ranch down the valley.

Upon returning we might find him clambering on the steering wheel or fooling with the directional-light bar. Once he found the horn button and used it, and once he found the headlights switch on the dashboard and turned them on.

He did not give up his human association easily, even briefly. There was no "explaining" to him that work must go on, in spite of his need to help. As with an infant, *his* needs were the universe's center, and *his* desires came first. And they were passionate ones! It was difficult to imagine, sometimes, so much *ego* poured into such a compact little carcass, but there it was, as undeniable as Tiger Mountain.

On days when spring rains which make the Western Cascades a green jungle also made the ropes and belts slip on their pulleys so the mill carriage would not move properly, we used the horses to skid more logs to the landing. In this instance Mister B.'s "help" also aided him in resolving whatever ponds of resentment at being stomped off horse legs were dammed up in his "subconscious."

On rainy days it was always like dawn or early dusk in the woods . . . a darkening place, the boughs all interlaced and meeting overhead. The places where the team had to go—or the horse alone, while the mare was tied up nearby —were like tunnels instead of trails.

The horse would move up efficiently to the dead-end of a trail, to where the down, bucked logs were, and prepare to turn himself around in what was usually a tight spot, when *out* from around a tree trunk he faced would come a monkey-like paw followed by Mister B.'s nose and glistering right eye.

"Snort!": the stampede of platter-sized hoofs; singletree and chain chattering like an ape's teeth in frenzy.

Back would duck Mister B. A quick skritching on the far side of the tree and he would lean around and out again, from nine feet up, just above the horse's head.

"Whoa. Hold up there," said Bill, who talked to the horse continuously and helped him to a feeling of half-security where this woods demon was concerned. It took more than a "whoa" sometimes. Mister B. had a habit of going up along the woods trails ahead of the horse, disappearing on a side trip, and then appearing from either side of the trail with an upthrust, "Watch yourself!" look. He operated silently, seeming to realize that this was more effectively scary than making a noise.

At such a time, loaded or not, the horse might run, harness chains jangling, neck arched, and nostrils fogging. If he ran before being hitched onto a log, he had to be followed out and led back. Mister B. would gallop along to aid in the capture, and follow back, whining a little self-satisfied war-whoop song.

A calming "whoa" never had much effect on the mare. She would roll her eyes wildly, step back over the traces and if possible get the singletree between her back legs, and take off, stumbling and banging herself into new hysteria with each lunge. "Let me *outta' here!*" She had never learned that work and horses go together (although she certainly knew that hay and horses *do*), and her life was one large one-ton vortex of work-escape mechanisms. She looked dull as a dinosaur about life, but about work she was actually as sly as a delinquent with a screwdriver in a used-car lot after midnight. For her, Mister B. was like spring tonic, and she worked her hysteria routine at his appearance as sedulously as a con-man with a time-tested pitch. Or, if she was tied to a tree, she would threaten to wrench it out or to hang herself whenever Mister B. appeared above her in the lower limbs.

The horse got used to him, after a fashion. Still, it always "bugged" him that Mister B. could be safely placed on the ground one moment and *appear* on a limb fifteen feet overhead the next: a black, moving *something*, probably with a scent that spelled "Danger! look out!" in the woods. Then, in a rapid slide-down which sounded as if it should have been accompanied by a shower of bark splinters, Mister B. would descend the backside of the tree and prepare to shout a silent "Boo!" That was always good for a snort and a horsy look askance. And a bear laugh, no doubt: "Buck me off, will you, when I make an honest mistake and climb your old leg!"

Even when my work was mental, Mister B. tried to keep

a paw in. He could not bear to have me sit still at my writing table. He climbed and clawed his way over me, the bookshelf, and the table top indiscriminately.

The conformation and sounds of the typewriter intrigued him, as they do, also, the small human animal; and whenever he climbed to the work table (a mahogany door bolted to cast-iron legs), he bee-lined for that infernal machine. He was "all over it" immediately. But, unlike archie the cockroach, he never mastered its workings. With forepaws on the keyboard he soon had all the striking arms meshed together, and his typing was over for the day. Then the mawling began. He walked up the keyboard and onto the carriage, wrenching the paper that was always in the machine to pieces, beginning at an upper corner and ripping downward with his teeth.

He actively—tooth, snarl, and claw—resented being removed from his busywork. Set firmly upon the floor, he would forthwith climb pants leg, chest, forearm of his host to the typewriter again, and again actively *resent* removal. I put him into the closet and slid the doors shut—then tried to "think" above his crescendoing wail, which was like that of woman for her demon lover. Then he was grasped firmly from behind, like a crab, and set outside where, backed into an undereaves corner of the house, his wails subsided into maundering snivels and snorts.

Was each minor rejection an agonizing re-enactment of the initial major rejection by his mother? Or was his reaction merely a manifestation of his eternal need for closeness? Having tried to understand a disturbed child, I tried, equally ineffectually, to understand Mister B. in the light of his "background." Looking back across an interval of time, I think he simply wanted to be the focus of full attention, just as the child had: the big "I" was his problem, just as it is any egoistic individual's.

If he could not participate during the day's typing, he tried to make up for it at night. I stood his inroads for a while, but soon began sending him outside at night, where he shared a corner of the front patio with Stella, a puppy of beagle-cocker parentage. Small as he was, Stella was smaller, and they cuddled together beyond my bedroom window. In the dark I could hear Mister B. nuzzling the puppy's belly, going m-mmm-mum-mimmmmm-mmm for ecstatic intervals, telling a monotonous bedtime story. When her skin stretched too tautly, Stella switched from plaintive whine to *screech*, and the bear would cease. But only momentarily. To this day, in adulthood, Stella has what might be termed a s-t-r-e-t-c-h-e-d stomach.

If nights happened to be sultry, as they are sometimes even in May, and the study windows were left open, Mister B. might tire of nuzzling Stella, sneak around the house, and clamber up five feet from the back patio to the sill. He used his back and feet to clamber up between one-inch boards covering the cracks where the rough cedar-siding boards met, worming his way like a mountain climber up a rock chimney. He would hoist himself over the window sill, edge inside, walk along the inside sill, hop down onto a bureau, turn backward, and drop to the floor. Then onto the typewriter chair, up to the table, and after the typewriter! Mission, momentarily at least, accomplished.

The laborious outside climbing I could observe in daylight when sometimes his furry rounded ears, beady eyes, and golden nose would appear, in a silence following the sound and fury of upward motion, over the sill. He would gaze for a moment, breathing heavily, and emerge inward.

84

Woe betide the "thinker" who grabbed him and tried to head him back out. He would spread all his feet against the sill and push, struggle, and *yow-l-l-l,* meanwhile tipping his head around and backward, mouth open and fangs gleaming.

One morning I found the window sill, which had never been tidied up since shortly after we built the house, *clean.* Vases, figurines, bird wings, pencils and note pads, seed pods and mountain-beaver skulls littered the bureau top and floor. Mister B., the new broom, had passed, radically.

Another morning, under the dark side of midnight, I dreamed I heard the typewriter going. In the morning I discovered the keys jammed, the desk papers and books collected into new piles, and Mister B. peacefully asleep in a nest of manuscript. His nose nested between his forepaws and, as I watched, one eye opened innocently. His rearranging was not so catastrophic as a housekeeper's neatness, but still intolerable. After that it was window and door securely *shut* for the workroom.

With even the most mundane of household chores, he helped. But sometimes he was as effectively disenchanting in his efforts as a young visitor, three-year-old Chuckie, who liked to feed the chickens until the scratch barrel ran dry. When the clothes were being hung out, Mister B. would start at one end of the line and go down, taste-testing towels, sheets, T-shirts, and work shirts. The larger, most get-aholdable ones were his favorites, and soon they all hung by one pin or rested on the grass below the line. He didn't mess around in them, once on the ground; and he used his paws in such a way that, thoughtfully enough, holes were not ripped in them.

Inside the house and out Mister B.'s cubhood help was

often, like that of the small, lavish-handed chicken-feeder, singularly unhelpful. There would be times in the future when both youngsters, maturing in their own patterns, would make me wish to have them nearby again, offering, wholeheartedly, their own peculiar helping hands.

IX *A Walk to the Creek*

Mister B. had an almost polar-bearish affinity for water, his only requirement being freshness. He turned his snout up at a hint of brackishness. Water did not have to be running, however, for if it was not, he would soon "flow it" aplenty with his paws, the ripples spreading out from him and lapping the edges of whatever pool or puddle, whether of man's or nature's making, he favored.

His bathing habits began in early cubhood when Bill first put him into the bathtub. Before he had the strength and stature to climb its slippery edge, he had to be lifted in. Once in the cool, shallow water, he would puff from one end to the other—snorting, splashing, or sitting up suddenly to examine his chest with one wet forepaw and watch the water drip from his top half; sometimes he sat with the dignity of a Buddha carved from obsidian; sometimes he raised his head and made nasal notes of maudlin ecstasy.

To be humane, and to keep the drain from clogging, stranded crickets had to be removed before the water was run in. He would clutch at the human valet's back leg throughout the readying process, with whines of: "Herd the crickets out of the bathtub, Mother, I want to sing in there myself." (He was always in a hurry to perform whatever was being suggested; always impatient to "get on with it," like any child; like a child, too, his enthusiasm for the current activity could terminate abruptly.)

Later, when he had to be out of the house most of the time, he retained pleasant memories of the bathtub. A child, visiting here with her parents, was told to take a bath. She returned to the living room, clutching her robe, leaned upon her mother's arm, and complained audibly: "I *would* take a bath, but some little boy's been walking around in there with dirty feet."

I slid away to perform a not-unfamiliar function—mopping the bear tracks out of the bathtub. The window was open a few inches and I could see that Mister B. had, as usual, clambered up, switched around on the sill, hung by his front feet, and dropped to the bathroom floor. He had hopped into the tub and probably sipped water from the slight declivity around the drain, then marched up and down the porcelain coolness. His feet, dusty from the ground outside, had left a scattering of tracks.

He had probably stood there for a while, forearms hanging over the edge of the tub, considering the other recreational possibilities of the bathroom. Then he had bowled with the cleanser can and played marbles with the round, white, porcelain knobs that covered the tops of bolts which held another bathroom fixture down. Finally, he had climbed the washbowl, s-t-r-e-t-c-h-e-d to reach the window sill, and left. Had the bathroom door been open, he would have ambled into the inner caves of the house, and have been "let out" or have wreaked havoc, depending upon whether or not humans were inhabiting the inner rooms at the time.

As I mopped up, I could "see" him, as I had many times upon opening the bathroom door, standing up in the tub, resting his forearms comfortably over the broad rim, like a housewife plumping her sudsy arms over a back-yard fence, his eyes as beady-bright and as innocent, in the dim light, as Satan's.

Then he would have said "Uuumph" or "Gnoomph" and put his arms up, as in infanthood, to be lifted out, his hind feet going slith-slith on the tub's slick surface.

I put the mop rag away, wound the window shut, and let the fastidious tot's mother know: "It's a trackless tub." She might never grow up to appreciate the singular honor of bathing with bear tracks.

The cow waterer which Bill installed in the pasture was a bear tub, too, only there no one mopped out tracks or ever felt constrained to do so. It was half a fifty-gallon oil drum placed inside the pasture fence on one side of the driveway. A water line led down from the main line in the field above and a spigot stood above the drum.

One hot mid-July day a neighbor drove in, dust on his black Cadillac, to bid us good-by before his ship sailed for Chile. He stood by the fence, where I had just filled the waterer, and looked out toward Tiger Mountain as he talked. In midsentence his speech was punctuated with a Gargantuan splash. Mister B., coming out from inspecting the car's undercarriage, had hoisted himself up and plunked into the cows' water. Waves lapped up and over the drum rim as he dunked himself riotously. His eyes glinted above his open mouth.

"Run for the camera," the neighbor said; but I preferred to share in the bear's original ecstasy as he rinsed himself by dunking clear down to the nostrils, then rising up again.

He stood up on the bottom, put his forepaws on the edges, shook, splashed, drank, snorted, cavorted.

The drum became his pasture spa, a watering-place half-way between house and creek. When he used it, he first nosed the air to determine if the coast was clear cow-wise. Then he hoisted himself up, got all four feet on the barrel's rim, pointed his hind end at the middle of the pool, looked back over his shoulder to see that he was aiming correctly, and let go with weighty abandon. The *splash* seemed to be as satisfying as the bath that followed. He did not believe in "total immersion," just almost-total. He took whole-bodied pleasure in the simple occupation of bathing, just as Adam probably took complete enjoyment from the first apple; there was no "original" (or subsequent) "guilt" in anything Mister B. did.

Many voyages later the seagoing neighbor was still recalling: "Boy, we should have had us a movie camera on that day when the bear discovered the cows' water."

On the front lawn Mister B. had a tub which was strictly his own: an enameled pan, once used in canning. Rectangular, it measured ten by sixteen inches, and was six inches deep. We filled it for him at first, and as a cub he could take a few breast strokes in it. Later, if we left the hose running and the nozzle off, he could fill his own tub, sitting up in it and holding the hose-end in one or both forepaws. With the hose he had as many variations of action as a baton twirler, holding it over his back, down his front, pointed into the tub or onto his head, meanwhile taking sips and "singing."

As summer's berries burgeoned and he fattened up, it became increasingly difficult for him to fit into his tub. The time came when he had to shoehorn himself in with a fat squishy splash that squeezed out nearly all the water. He would lean back against one end, his hind feet and legs out the other end, touching ground, and only his backside immersed. Or, he would sit up straight and contemplate his navel, like Buddha, dabbing delicately with one paw's toe-nails at the ribbon of water outlining his stomach. The hair of his backside and wrists got wet—that's all.

He could not believe he had outgrown the tub, just as a man cannot believe he is no longer loved when he still loves. "How can this *be?*" both say. Both refuse to believe it, and as long as they can get close to the object of their affection, they get as close as they can. Alas, the juice is almost all out of it.

As a youngster, bathing thus, Mister B. did not appreciate comment and pointing on the part of visitors, and would shoot them dirty looks while they shot film. Maturing, he became more complacent about the matter and bathed before visitors with less sense of offended dignity: "Whatever will be, will be."

During the early summer I spent a portion of some days felling and sawing into firewood lengths some of the broad-leaved maple and red-alder trees by a swamp east of the house in a loop of the Tiger Mountain Road. The swamp, fed by springs bubbling from the side hill and under stumps, had always been a sanctuary for wildlife, mainly birds which fed upon the berries of dogwood and cascara trees growing there. Evergreen trees hedged it on the high land along the road, and we hoped to make it into a long, shallow pond to attract more wild creatures. Besides the birds, it was already home to frogs, toads, and salamanders. Deer lived and had their young in the thickets by its upper end. Once I had seen a small black bear spurt out across the main road as I was coming down, and knew that he had been berrying or gouging up the roots of skunk cabbages which grew to jungle-lush proportions in the swamp muck.

While I cleared the fruitless "weed" trees, Mister B. swished desultorily through some of the puddles there, but they were muddier than he preferred and the black soil got on his hair tips and dried. He combed at it with his claws, but then tried to get to fresh, running water as quickly as possible in order to cleanse himself properly. In this regard he remained, as I suppose wild bears must be, fastidious. They appear to sweat only on the nose, like hogs, but unlike hogs will not abide much mud on the hide. (As a matter of fact, unpenned hogs prefer clean water, too, and a huge Duroc boar we once let roam—until we found him to be sliding up behind chickens and eating them alive—would go to the creek on hot days. I would come upon him there, marching silent circles in the water, only his back out, moving ponderously, like a hippopotamus.)

A neighbor's boy, about eleven, came daily to where I cleared, to help a little and then to climb trees with Mister B. But in the heat of the day the two youngsters would prevail upon me to go swimming in the creek. Our favorite hole was a basin upstream from the waterfalls, at the upper end of a canyon sliced through solid andesite rock. Eons of running water had smoothed a trough slanting into it, a slide which made entree easy and, once one had begun to slide, inevitable.

On our first day there, in early July, the boy slid in and I followed—first shaking loose Mister B.'s clawhold on my shoulder. Mister B. was still tiny at the time and he hit the slide immediately after me and landed swimming, mostly under water. As I looked to one side, there he was, paddling for dear life. In the deep pool he v-ed, only nose and eyes and top of head above water. He had always been tub-paddling before, never swimming; but he took to deep water like a veteran.

After a few minutes I turned purple and escaped to a shaft of sunlight above the pool. But the boy had warmer blood and the bear a thicker hide. They gamboled like porpoises, save that Mister B. kept his eyes and nose above the water.

There was a man who had mineral claims in the hills nearby. He pointed, once, to a high ridge where he said that he had found a sackful quantity of jade—dropped, he surmised, from a partially extant logging-railroad trestle by whoever had been carrying it. He gave us specimens and it *was* jade, although not of as high quality as Wyoming jade. He had searched for but never found the mother lode—if, indeed, there was a mother lode at all and not just a boulder which the earlier prospector had broken up for easier carrying. But had I happened upon a minor mountain of jade up there along the familiar skyline, it would not have brought half the pure enjoyment of swimming with the bear. We have all seen bears in their ablutions in zoos, in everything from antique brown-ringed bathtubs to cement pools a quarter-acre in extent, and have enjoyed, from outside the bars, their obvious delight with even tepid and more-than-twice-used water. To actually *share* the bear's pleasure next one's own hide in green, pure, almost snow-cold water—that's living.

As I watched, a kingfisher flew over, racketing like a rusty wrench, his pinion feather-ends all separate against the sky. From downstream came a water ouzel, whirring along about two feet above the creek's surface. Chittering a

blunt, loud note in time to the machine-gun beat of its
blunt wings, he or she (both ouzel sexes are the same slate
gray, save that Audubon saw frail white markings at the
outer tips of the large feathers of the male's wing) braked
to a stop on a wet rock at stream center above me. With its
peculiar bobbing motion, taking deep-knee-bends and chattering, the ouzel observed the intruders in its creek. Then
it walked down the face of its observation rock and went
completely under water, to search for periwinkles on the
stream's floor.

"Life consists of wildness. The most alive is the wildest,"
Thoreau said. The water ouzel is his maxim personified.
From first breakout of its white eggshell, in a nest which
may be sprayed by cascading water or even set behind the
crystal curtain of a waterfall, to an adulthood spent always
in, under, and near pure water, the ouzel enjoys an exist-
ence wild and Spartan. Joy there must be, for it makes
music even winterlong when snow puffs the creek rocks
and icicles stalk the banks. Whether its song be a series of
thrushlike trills, a rich and intricate melody, or merely a
jibbering twitter to pass the time and scare away the cold,
the ouzel is a poet. A happy one.

The ouzel whizzed past me, going back downstream,
silent now, its beak bristling with a mustache of periwinkles.
It must have young. They would be standing up in the nest,
or on rocks in the stream, crying one piercing note like the
shriek of water sprites come to life. When it brought the
food, the young ones would whir-r-r their stubby wings as
they gulped. A moment later they would be shrieking
"More!"

Seeing one of our several ouzels was always sufficient re-
ward for a walk to the creek. Full twenty years, when not

away at sea, I have always gone to the creek the first thing in the morning. At first it was with buckets; for five years, before the power line was extended up the mountain, the creek was the household's "running water." Psychologically profound visitors from the country's centers of culture said that I carried water because I had a "guilt complex." My failure to agree undoubtedly convinced them that I had, additionally, a "subconscious need to suppress a guilt complex." I thought of it as a simple need-for-water complex— and, growing out of that, a need-to-walk-to-the-creek complex. Whatever it may be, it is there to stay, and nothing will "psychologize" it out of my pattern of living.

Clean water, like the air, gives life. A stream is like an open artery, gushing crystal, and to it come any region's animals and birds: to drink, to feed and bathe, and then—since the joy of life wells in replete animals more spontaneously than in humans—to cavort. When they are not physically present, they leave their marks: the sand-skrit of songbirds; the bold, primary, stylus marks of herons; the butter-print-perfect marks of minks; the bounding-away or browsing v's of deer; the human hand-prints of raccoons, which seem to hold a drop of innocent laughter in each impression.

The marks of tragedy are there, too, for a temperate-zone creek is a place of danger, sometimes, if not of the violently-colored drama of the jungle water hole. One sees the spilled blood and scattered entrails of minor tragedies (major enough, to the participants). But, then, the blood draws butterflies—and life is full of rainbow hues all over again.

At the creek the seasons make their first appearance and their last stand. Here the plant the pioneers called wild rhubarb first unfolds its star-shaped leaves in February and here the broad, ribbed leaves of cascara and alder hang on some years until almost Christmas. By regarding the creek closely one truly sees the year's calendar—tears off the days, as it were. The hours are written in water and sand similarly year by year, but never twice exactly the same, with all the nuances from joy to anger, from nourishment—of soil, plant, and animal—to their destruction in times of the creek's raging or of an animal battle fought there. There is not much mineral gold in the creek and it takes hours to pan out a few cents' worth of colors; but there is truly the gold of living, in quantities to confound a Midas.

So, mornings, I had always gone to the creek. And, doing so, I "owned" the world: it was all mine. When I had living with me a foster child who would not be weaned from his childhood patterns of what society calls delinquency, I went to the creek alone, before he awoke, and it became my only time of peace and reassurance in each day.

But Mister B. made it a duality: I could never arise and go without his hearing me and following. Or leading. *We* went to the creek together; we both loved it; it was *our* creek.

Sometimes he got there ahead of me, and down zoomed the dragonfly or up lifted, in angular slow-motion and trailing hinged stilts of legs, the great blue heron. Or, other times, up skimmered the kingfisher. The heron, kingfisher, and water ouzel, all seekers-along-the-stream and all having predominant elements of gray-blue in their plumage, were yet so different in habits and body structure as to seem to belong to different "races" of animals altogether.

One time the kingfisher had dropped a troutlet, three inches long, and it was dying, lying on its side in the shallow water so that it was glistening gold, not invisible and dark-camouflaged as it would have been normally, idling,

[12] *He could not believe that he no longer fit the pan in which he had bathed as a cub.*

[13] Above, *Mister B. enjoying a favorite snack, red huckleberries, in his favorite position.*

[14] Below, *another favorite: raspberries, savored one by one.*

[15] Above, *Mister B. and one of his best friends, the rooster.*
[16] Below, *"wrestling" with Bill.*

[17] *Edging his way into the house.*

head upstream. Mister B. saw it and claw-tipped at it, but without putting his nose under water or holding it. Then he went on, spurting a bit, to make up for time lost in such trifling.

Sometimes, like Thoreau, he could spend all morning near the doorway, "wrapped in a reverie"; but there were other times when, feeling that he might miss something of importance around the next bend in the road or in the day, he ran forward, almost frantically, in order to keep up with time's passing.

It seems to me that this full acceptance of our world is the only way we humans and other animals "put it over" on time—counteract, in our own pygmy existences, the overpowering nature of earth's age and ability to outlive us. In such small ways as walking to the creek daily, and dwelling there for a breathing space, we spear upon experience's tines and bring to our spirits' mouths our own small morsels of eternity, which, once we have tasted, can never be taken from us.

And the morsels shared are *forever* shared. I know that. I do not walk to the creek these mornings alone, for Mister B. goes with me, just as do the other beings, mortal and immortal, who have gone that way with me before, and those who walk there sometimes in these present seasons, and those who will come after.

X *Bear Mechanic*

We have heard of the feral child, a human reared by animals or by himself in a state of nature. Once introduced to society, such a child has everything to learn; the heritage of humankind comes at him full-blast: language, customs, tools, artifacts—the whole intricate web of living, as "people" do it.

Mister B. became civilized the same way (although he never overcame the feral child's predilection for going sometimes on all fours, sometimes erect). In the process he showed a mechanical attitude, even aptitude. Young animals, like children, customarily (before likes and dislikes develop) "take to" everything presented to them in their universe. A strictly "wild" bear would not have an opportunity to know motors; but one could not say that he did not like motors—only that he had not seen one.

From the first Mister B. loved gadgets, tools, and machines. Cars, especially. Sometimes it seemed that he tried to get as "close" to cars as he did to living creatures. When he had been in a human house little more than a week, he was already climbing over, under, and through my blue, 1953, six-cylinder Ford. He brought to "her" that combination of possessiveness, protectiveness, and devotion which it had taken me years to develop and which I had not felt for any other car.

She was the plainest model; yet, through long association, I fell in love with her. She did my work on the rural mail route and she ran errands across the state on free-lance assignments (she appeared, once, in the *Saturday Evening Post's* "So We Commemorate," standing in the foreground at Samuel Hill's replica of Stonehenge). In her back-seatless area she carried a whiteface calf home from the Snohomish Auction and wriggly wild pigs down from Fall City. She had carried friends to busses, planes, and trains for meetings and leavings. Life's arrivals and departures—she knew them all. She had known the anguish of more than a year's weekly trips to a state reformatory, and the subdued happiness of the last trip there, when the gates finally opened for the child I had visited.

I did not feel, for my Ford, that sexy adoration which many American men feel, nor that substandard-godliness which youth assumes for itself when girded with "wheels," but, rather, a good solid comfort and loyalty.

So was she close to the tiny bear heart. With upreaching arms he hoisted his four-pound frame to the front bumper, up to the fender, trod the hood across to the windshield, scrambled onto the window ledge . . . and once inside, went back and forth across the seats. He crawled under the seats and took inventory of the small tools there, sometimes falling asleep with a wrench between his paws, his chin resting on it. I became accustomed to reaching for a tool and touching bear fur. His eyes would open brightly and his tongue unfurl as he yawned: "Is this what you're looking for?" I kept a clean rag handy for wiping his telltale footprints off the hood and car top, the leatherette seat covers, and the dashboard before going to town.

Why did he hanker for the car? There was nothing in it for him, except the faint perfume of extant groceries, the mealy smells of dairy feed, and the sweet dust of dried corn that had been hauled home from the Co-op. Yet in and all around he must go. Partly it was the climbing exercise he needed and this mechanical tree was his gymnasium, his substitute for woods-work. Partly the car was like a home for him, a pleasure-dome. It was, too, a place that his human friends frequented. But, more than that, he had an attitude toward it which other animals, wild or domestic, did not have, and which I can only describe as being one of mechanical aptitude. He "took to" the car in a friendly and unharried manner; inside a week or two he had an at-homeness with it which it had taken me years to develop.

When he got ready to leave the car, he climbed the arm-rest to the window ledge, hung down by one forepaw (he always descended backward), and tried to touch ground with a back paw. Of course he couldn't. Then, back up to the ledge to peer down to gauge the drop, muttering to himself; then, to try touching ground again. As a youngster, he would not drop. So there was nothing for it but to explore the car all over again inside, then to try for the ground again, as if the distance might have lessened by that time. (In this simple detail, as in many others, he recalled my own mental blocs and eccentricities to me: wait awhile; pretend it didn't happen; then look again, and presto, the world will surely have come round, the problem be solved! But, of course, it is never thus.)

Car-climbing helped him to develop what was soon to be a tremendous strength, particularly in the forearms. He could let himself down full-length and bring his body weight up again, one-armed. Within a few weeks I could feel the bulge of arm muscles that seemed to be almost as large as his body and more solid.

He loved to help anyone working under a car or truck. He would paw and mouth the tools, then walk along the frame members and axles, often standing directly over the mechanic's face and kicking down a trickle of oily dirt accumulations. Told to "move on!" he would argue plaintively and, if pushed, screech. "I'm helping; you'd better appreciate it!"

After such a session, when he had his head under my chin, nuzzling, and I put my nose to his fur, he smelled like a grease-monkey. Other times he smelled like fir-tree pitch. These were the only odors I could detect on him. Young bears are practically odorless; with older males, like older pigs, or men who need a "man-sized deodorant," it is not so.

The motor sounds of the Ford and the pickup truck were well known to him. All his young life he disappeared into the garage or around the house when he heard a strange motor coming in from the main road. Then, depending upon our own attitudes toward the visiting vehicle, he would re-appear or not. If we visited with the stranger, he might suddenly emerge and begin climbing the wheels and under-carriage of the vehicle; he would not go inside, however, and it was several months before he would go up the hood and over the top of strange cars. Sometimes he would not appear at all; he seemed to have a sixth sense which told him when to keep hidden and when he would be welcome. I believe that voices had much to do with it. A bellowing or cantankerous voice sounded danger to him; a quiet one, acceptance. Whenever Ellen came, her voice and her pickup's motor said "Peace be with you" to him. When she departed, she always looked under her truck to be sure he was out of the way. "Once we had to tug him out from under the hood three times before I could leave," she said. "We would take him out and he would duck right back in. Bill finally had to hold him till I left the yard."

His love of my car helped him to develop an early maturity in his sleeping arrangements. Overnight, and altogether on his own, he built himself a den there.

During mid-June I carried the rural mail on Route 2 out of Issaquah regularly. Before starting for the post office in the sunlit but still-cool dawn, I always lifted the car's hood to check the oil. One morning when I reached for the dip stick, two beady eyes gazed up innocently. Mister B. looked up with a certain sly insouciance: "Who's disturbing my den?"

Then I saw that he had neatly removed all the rock-wool insulation glued under the hood on the left side, and had rearranged the material to form a nest between the fender and the engine block. There he cuddled, in a mechanical den, with a warm motor (at least the first part of the night) for mother. I removed the bear, then the batting. He retired, muttering and mumbling, to the patio corner where he had slept with the puppy all spring.

When I brought the car home from the route that day, I left the hood up in order to do some minor tuning-up; at least one plug was misfiring, and with nearly five hundred stops a day, it was a waste of gas and of peace-of-mind, too. (A man who had taken the route as substitute once, years before, had simply returned to the office from halfway around, dumped what was left of the daily mail, and said,

"I quit." Halfway around, every day, I knew how he felt, and that was pressure enough without the added concern: *can* the car make it?)

My job was incomplete by suppertime, so I left the hood up, gaping like an alligator's jaw. When I went out after supper there stood Mister B., back feet firmly on the right fender, head and nose pointed up, front paws busily picking at the under-hood insulation. Like a swallow, he was preparing to rebuild his damaged nest. He had a real sense of order about mechanical things, so that while he removed the batting, he did it neatly and completely and from only one side of the hood; and he never once tore into the upholstery of the seats or the foam rubber.

His habit of motorized slumber might have led to his decapitation in a whirling fan blade. I sorted the afternoon's incoming mail each evening in order to keep up with the onslaught of every next-morning's incoming flood. On June 22, after supper, and not realizing that Mister B. had already retired, I started for the post office, six miles away.

Where Tiger Mountain Road joins the Hobart Road, the gas pedal gave an unnatural lurch. What now? I thought. The answer came when, a mile beyond, I heard a loud *Waaaaaah!*—unmistakably Mister B. I pulled off to the side and raised the hood. There he stood on his hind legs where the fender meets the frame, both front paws up, his mouth oozing a bubble of supper-milk and his eyes black with grief. He held his forepaws to be lifted. I picked him up and he clutched me around the neck, thrusting like a plumber's helper to attach his mouth, nuzzling my neck and cheek.

I got in, whirled the car around and sped for home. On the way I met a neighbor who looked up askance from his gleaming sports car at the sight of two heads behind the steering wheel. Mister B. continued his frantic nuzzling all the way home.

"Bears aren't cuddly," Lois Crisler had told me. Lois and her husband, Herb, had photographed bears in the Olympic Mountains of Washington and throughout Alaska. No, they aren't, but they demand affection and need it in times of stress, and this was one of Mister B.'s distress times.

While he continued for some weeks to sleep alongside the motor, he now waited to retire until after the evening mail was sorted.

He learned about cars the hard way for the second time two days later. Bill went for the mail at the box across from the main gate on Tiger Mountain Road, thinking that he had successfully ditched Mister B., for we did not want him to get into the habit of going toward the road.

But he had heard Bill. He emerged suddenly from a thicket of brake ferns beside the gate and dashed out into the road. "A car was coming up, thirty or forty miles an hour," Bill said. "It hit him with the right front wheel and bounced him clear off to the side. The kid driving stopped; he was sorry about it."

Mister B. appeared to be dead when Bill picked him up. "He wasn't breathing, but then I felt his heart beating."

Bill laid him on the grass in front of the house, where he remained unconscious for an hour or more. This, his only "hibernation," was as inadvertent as it was unseasonal. That night I fed him strawberries. His jaw hurt so that he couldn't cope with a whole berry but had to have it cut in pieces and slipped between his teeth. His right front leg was at an unusual angle, but not broken or even lumpy. He didn't do much climbing of trees in the woods for the next few days, but would just stand on his hind legs and embrace them at the base, gazing nostalgically upward. Within a week he was climbing again, but not with the rush and exuberance of his springtime climbing.

While he did not lose interest in machinery as he grew older, he became more deliberate in his "work." Just as he did not try so often to prove that he could outrun the dogs on the woods roads, so he did not leap to help so quickly when a mechanic was working. His increasing girth made it a tight fit in his nest slung between the engine block and fender, and he stopped using that oil-and-grease-scented den.

He still loved to rearrange tools wherever they were laid out, delicately scrambling them, like a dental assistant gone hysterical. He discovered and thoroughly studied all appendages of vehicles. Windshield wipers became his favorites. He would sit on the hood solemnly regarding his reflection in the windshield. (In mid-July, while watching him look at himself in this outdoor mirror, I noticed that he was beginning to grow a ruff under his lower jaw, about a third of the way back from his jaw tip; it gave him the distinguished look of an elder bear statesman.) After having examined his reflection he would remove one or both of the wipers, using teeth and one paw, delicately. On some cars it was easy; on others, a complex process. When he had one or both wipers laid out neatly on the hood, he would give a satisfied groan and scramble down over the fender. To this day, the pickup's right wiper, a replacement for one that he did not remove quite carefully enough, does not work properly.

At least he tried. He had unusual willingness and above-average dexterity. And, given proper tutelage, he might have become an A-1 mechanic.

XI *Berrying*

With the advent of berrypicking time, in late June and early July, Mister B.'s built-in grouchiness eased. It may have been only his maturation, but I think that it had to do with berries and with the act of garnering them.

One cannot be tense in a berry patch, the sun hot on the neck's nape, the hands busy among the bushes, and juice sweet on the lips. Small birds—wild canaries, juncos, and song sparrows—fly up from their nests in low forks. Quail cry from the fence rows. Ruffed grouse chicks whir-r-r away, following their mothers.

Some of the most peacefully satisfying times of my youth are concerned with warm berry fields, the strawberry rows and raspberry hedges, the festooned curves of vine loaded with loganberries. Berrypicking times were to be among the best of Mister B.'s days too.

One late June morning we were crossing the creek when I realized that the salmonberries—which had been in their state of deep-lavender bloom only a day before, it seemed—were ripe. As with every growing thing, the ripening appeared to have happened overnight. And perhaps it had. The fruit—sometimes yellow, sometimes red-orange—glittered at

the tips of boughs extending beyond the green-black leaves,
the thorn-barbed stems and stemlets.

Out of long habit I reached and tasted, savoring the not-
tart, not-very-sweet, not-much-of-anything, but unmistakable
ripe-berry lusciousness between tongue and palate. Up
reared Mister B. on his hind legs with his "gimme-some,
too" groan.

I gathered half a palmful as quickly as possible, goaded
by his eternal impatience, and, upcupping my hand, presented them. He nose-dived in and the palm was wiped
clean. I could see him mushing them around between his
own purple tongue and pink palate, getting the taste.

The work that lay farther upland, in the form of cedar
logs to be split into fence posts, would have to wait while
we went a-berrying, I could see. While I moved around the
outer edges of the salmonberry thickets, he stood up against
the back of my leg and groaned his demands: "Can't you
speed this up?" The berries do not grow thickly and, no, I
could not speed it up. I told him so.

He followed me upstream, sometimes stooping to test a
grass blade or to tongue a warm rock's mineral surface, but
mostly he had a one-track, berry-set mind; I could almost
peer into his convoluted brain and see there a huge, yellow,
juice-glistening salmonberry, as luscious as a seaman's mental pin-up girl.

My hands brought the berries down while he clung: both
paws around one leg; or one forepaw hanging down and
the other just resting upon the leg walking stick; or one paw
leaning out and one raised upward, like the palm of an in-
satiate panhandler. Occasionally he would stand clear on his
hind feet, one forearm dangling, one up.

"Well, now, you can learn this for yourself," I told him,

and bent a bough-tip berry down until it rubbed his snoot. He took it ungraciously. The second one he took even more slowly. The third he sniffed at before accepting.

"*You* can do it a lot faster, so cut the fiddle-faddle and get with it," he groaned at me.

"No, you're big enough to learn." I bent a bush out along the ground, put a rock on it and, picking him up, turned him and set him down along it. "Get to work."

He could have, but he wouldn't. Instead, like a recalcitrant child, he embraced my leg, looking up. "This isn't the way we started it, and I don't want to change the original setup."

Out of pure enjoyment of the situation as it stood, he was not going to shift over to salmonberry-picking on his own. His bottomless belly groaned for more and his jaws worked while he made *sotto-voce* moans. And so as we went along the creek, higher and higher, it appeared that we could go on all morning and nothing outstanding in the way of a change would occur.

It riled me. There were, as always, many things to do, some pressing (a valley farmer had ordered two hundred posts for delivery on the weekend), some merely necessary to the maintenance of a certain order in one's own small universe (although an outsider is sometimes unable to see evidence of any order whatsoever). There were the usual naggings which ride, like the Old Man from the Sea, on all our backs, however broad: fret of an inner insufficiency; money worries which no number of sold posts would ever quite set right; the ache for that youngster who had been like a son to me and who now could not or would not see that he was on a greased slide to catastrophe. Things that could be "fixed"; things that couldn't be; premonitions that hung like a small, gray cloud inside the rib cage. And there was as well the Puritan-Victorian upbringing which says, "Make every minute count"—for exactly *what*, I don't know, except that it "should" be filled with work or, at very least, with "improving one's self"—*getting something and hanging onto it*. Has anyone ever ascertained the cash value of a minute?

It had got so that, in my years on the ranch, I picked up something solid (molecules may all be in motion but, at least, it *felt* solid) every time I walked, so that any return to the house must be a *laden* return, whether it be with a tree limb for the fireplace or a rock for ringing the base of a garden tree or a cull post for use on the next fencing project or a piece of scrap cedar for making a picket.

But on this day—and it was one of many things that Mister B. taught *me* (while I was not particularly successful, that first day, at teaching *him* berrypicking)—I found that there is more to life than sticks, stones, and a healthy savings account . . . more, even, than "improving" the mind or composing a poem. All of which I had known, of course, but this was one of the first times I ever found it possible to *act* upon it . . . thanks to the bear. There is savoring the moment; there is bathing the winter-soiled spirit in pure, sunshiny air; there is shaking the soul's wrinkles out, until it comes smooth and smells fresh, like a clean sheet brought in from where it has been hanging in a summer wind.

So along the creek we went, up and up, releasing the frets like rusty moths and letting them puff upward until they were less than specks in the pellucid sky. Instead of picking something up to *clutch*, it was a time of opening the whole fist of being and letting life's botherations go: "Shoo, scat." They did. To "waste" a morning's sunlit hours in a pursuit of pure innocence was to save one's soul for a few more years.

Even Mister B.'s pressure against my legs (he was, as a probation officer had said of a juvenile type, "leaning on me") ceased to be a pressure and became something light as a tuft of rabbit fur. Lighter, even: a joy, not a job. Of course, I had always "known" this intellectually about berry-picking. Now I really knew it with my blood and bones. Mister B. felt it, too. On the way home he ran up behind me and nipped the calf of my leg in pure frolic, then rushed around me and led the way, gamboling like a puppy.

With the burgeoning of berries, however, the patterns of our lives diverged slightly. When he learned to pick for himself—which was soon—Mister B. began to locate bushes and patches, and to make his own small excursions.

After salmonberries, the ebony blackcaps set on, ripe in the tipmost branches first, delicious as forbidden fruit in their whorled clusters above the barbed and bluish main-stems. Mister B. shared them with the ground-nesting and low-nesting birds, so that sometimes I would see him standing and lipping at them delicately or tugging a paw pad from a thorn and moaning low to himself. Meanwhile, farther down along the bough would be a rusty song sparrow or a white-crowned sparrow viewing him with one eye while pecking at the fruit, either to eat it on the spot or to slip off the entire cap and fly it by fast-freight to a quartet of nestlings.

Simultaneously came the thimbleberries, bright as arterial blood in first gushing. Thimbleberries were more to the birds' taste than Mister B.'s, their color being the only thing about them not watery and insipid.

After July 4 the wild blackberries, black prince of all

stump-ranch fruit, ripened. Their full-flavored sweet-tartness and the smell their stain left on fingers and palms had been an element of my life since earliest youth. The first year here, 1941, I determined to put into effect the pioneer boast of "living off the land," and canned more than fifty quarts of them, representing many hours of picking, for they are tiny. And rich: visitors, eating them as sauce, would break out in perspiration.

Now, in the heat of a July forenoon when I went blackberrying, Mister B. followed, lagging a little behind in his own, grass-hidden berrybushes, surrounded by white, gold-centered daisies and a tall species of bitter-smelling dandelion. He panted like a dog, audibly, as the sun laid its full heat upon his glossily-black, heat-absorbent pelt.

Sometimes he would duck in under the shade of a fir tree, or slide down a grassy tunnel to behind the creek bank, where there are hundreds of mountain-beaver tunnel mouths and the ground, still halfway moist, made a cool couch.

But when I left the day's berry patch and headed home, he would be coming along behind—toeing-in, mouth open, and panting—having heard or felt from his hiding-nest in the cool the vibrations of my departure. He had less inclination than before to run to catch up and take a fun-nip at my leg.

With the advent of berries he seemed to be gaining half a pound a day, and suddenly he weighed between thirty and forty pounds. Apparently berries have a weight-making effect on the bear's internal apparatus that other foods do not.

After the days spent in the warm berry fields he had the same calmness of spirit that occurs in humans at such times. I regretted that I had not observed, as some of my Indian friends had, the gathering of a bear clan in berry fields to

picnic, with child-swatting, minor squabbling over who discovered which bush first, and napping between feastings—
just as humans do.

In July, also, the red elderberries, which ripen much earlier than blue elderberries and have smaller bushes, matured. Mister B. ate elderberries but did not bring to them
the orgy-like luxuriousness he devoted to blackberries.
When he came upon an elderberry bush it was usually by
accident, as when he followed the cows. Like all animals,
he enjoyed being where those of other species were, for he
liked company, though at a slight distance. The cowbell
seemed to be a bulwark of defense or of companionship to
him just as it is to humans working in their fields or waking
in the misty morning to the sound of grazing music and
slumbering peacefully again, for an interval of security, before arising.

One day I looked upcreek from the lower garden to where
the cowbell chuckled busily in the canary grass and saw
Mister B. lying out at full length, caterpillar-like, along a
bough, to get at red elderberries. He lay along the slender,
bamboo-like but rough-barked bough, moving farther and
farther out toward the flat, butter-dish-sized cluster of red
fruit. Each separate berry is tiny, but altogether they make
a beautiful bouquet. Just as his tongue reached the berries,
he fell out of the tree, ingloriously. He rolled himself upright, glared nearsightedly toward the sound of the cowbell,
whose ringing ceased abruptly, and *dashed* for the protectiveness of stumps and thickets hedging the field. When the
bell resumed, he edged back, whining and growling, and
tried again. But suddenly he appeared beside me and began climbing my shovel—an inveterate manipulator of man's
tools, as well as of his emotions. "This cow-following is an

insecure business, sometimes," he seemed to say. "Let me get back to something I am *sure* of."

Down along the creek canyon, below the garden's bench of sandy, alluvial soil, the alder and broad-leaved maple trees grow jungle-lush. A decade ago one caught glimpses of the creek when flying over in summertime, but now all one sees is a torrent of treetops pouring down the canyon. Down on the gravelly, boulder-strewn canyon floor and lapping up its sides there is a second jungle: salmonberry bushes, devil's walking club, Oregon grape, and red huckleberry.

Red-huckleberry leaves, oval, the size of chipmunk ears, turn pale green when sun shines through them. They spill lacy shadows on logs and the creek's surface, the bushes and their shadows together having the delicacy of Japanese impressionism. The bright pink berries, uniformly the size of salmon eggs, have been used by fishermen for catching trout. The berries are thick on the underside of the boughs, growing singly, not in clusters.

Puget Sound pioneers wrote Back East in the 1850s to report that "whortleberries are on the bushes until December"—to show the climate's mildness. I believe they referred to blue huckleberries which grow on tougher-foliaged, shiny-leaved bushes that florists use as backing for bouquets and for display pieces. Huckleberry brush-picking is a minor industry and brush-pickers work year-round at it. The red huckleberries ripen early and get wormy by late summer, their thin skins shriveling if they remain on the bush. The blue ones ripen later (at least, at sea level), their tougher skin making them better keepers.

Red huckleberries spring from taller main-stems. The bushes often sprout upward from the tops of stumps, rooting in the hollow centers, liking the rotting pith wood and the moisture which collects there and tolerating the elements of fir pitch. (In the days when pasture stumps were minor Mount Everests to us, my brothers and I used to drink from the pools of rain water atop pasture stumps, the aromatic taste of pitch coloring the drink—children, like small bears, being inveterate taste-testers in nature.)

At first Mister B. had to be shown the huckleberries, too. I bent the boughs to his nose; he sniffed, tongued, gobbled with minor pleasure-groans. When the bushes snapped erect, he could not understand where the fruit had gone. But soon his habit of stump- and log-climbing brought him to a closer relationship, and from then on he became a huckleberry connoisseur.

Their bushes made his every expedition a companioned one, for he could always stop off for a belly-filling tussle with a bush. Sometimes they provided him with a handy excuse for following humans. One hot, mid-July day my younger brother's family went swimming in the deep pool under the waterfalls downcreek. His wife, Jackie, reported: "Mister B. followed us at a distance. He looked down from the grove above the falls to see what we were doing. Then one of the children spotted him lurking up there and pointed at him. We all looked. Mister B. grabbed onto a huckleberry bush growing from a rock crevice up there and began to pick berries. He kept peering around the bush at us but whenever we looked back he began picking again as if to say: 'See, I'm minding my own business!'"

With huckleberries he always had "room for one more." When I would bring home a particularly heavily-laden branch from the woods, he would lie on his back in the grass near the front door and sort the berries off with his mouth, holding the branch with all four feet, the picture of utter bliss. The bottoms of his feet were, I noted, no longer smooth. Roughing-it in the blackberry patches had toughened and calloused them; and when I rubbed a finger across them I felt the innumerable barbed and scarred places—the ribbons of his berrying campaigns.

Of course, humans and bears do not always find peace together in the berry fields. My father tells of Grandpa Petite and a company of neighbor men who went, during the first years of this century, to Larch Mountain in southern Washington on a huckleberrying expedition. They took Grandpa's horse, Old Dixie, to carry camping equipment and to bring back the ten-gallon milk cans full of blue huckleberries. As they were returning, the horse ladened with ripe fruit, a berrying bear frightened the horse, who ran away, strewing berries. Grandpa and his friends, justifiably annoyed, added bear meat to the load. Grandpa, never one to overlook any aspect of an experience ("A Scotchman is Scotch, but a Frenchman will skin a flea," he once told me), added to the family income by writing up the episode for the Portland *Oregonian*.

More modern humans are not apt to be so provident. Several summers ago Bill and I flew to the Queen Charlotte Islands, a Canadian archipelago off the coast of British Columbia, across Hecate Strait from Ketchikan, Alaska. On Graham Island, the northern of the two main islands, on the road a few miles above the Indian village of Skidegate, we met an Indian boy with a high-powered rifle. What was he doing? "Looking for bears."

"Why?" we asked him. It was midsummer, not an appropriate season for hunting.

"Oh, sometimes the women are picking berries and they [the bears] come at them."

"To hurt them?" (It was before the time of Mister B. and I did not realize just how nearsighted bears are; the rustle of human activity might attract their eternal curiosity before the scent of humans frightened them off.)

"No, it scares the women. They come toward them."

"Do you use the bears for anything? Meat or fur?"

"No, nothing."

The boy was from the Mission at Skidegate. He had killed, and left to rot, four bears the previous summer, and "Only two, this year." He seemed ignorant of classic Indian teachings, a part of Indian religion, to hold animal life sacred, particularly where bears are concerned. In the Haida myths of his forefathers, bears were so closely akin to humans that they had taken Indian women to wife; some of the totems even depicted such an event. At any rate, an Indian hunter was enjoined by religion to use all parts of whatever animal he killed. It was a sign of respect. Elders among the Yakima Indians had told me: "If a hunter ever killed more than he could use, or did not use all that he killed, he was treated as a social outcast."

Superficially "Christianized," the young Indian hunter epitomized a fearsomeness which was neither Christian nor Indian. Unfortunately, we do not have Christ's commandment on bears, but I do not think it would have been "Shoot 'em."

Closer home, we heard from neighbors of a family who had sighted a bear and her cubs in a wild blackberry patch beyond their house. They had called all available departments of government and had had the bear family trapped, shot, or otherwise disposed of . . . and this with miles of uninhabited brushland country behind them. The bears had only to be shooed away and they would have gone (as Mister B.'s mother and sibling[s] had)—and would undoubtedly have effectively vanished within the space of a square mile or less. But, no, the poor humans could not keep "hands off"—nor could they conceive of their wild neighbors as one of life's minor miracles which they had fallen heir to: a treat to be enjoyed, not a threat to be destroyed. Whence this dire poverty of the modern human spirit? Who threatens you, pale heart, save only your own weak-spirited *self?*

Elders of the Yakima Indians, still living closely with nature, regard all its manifestations with respect, from roots and berries to salmon, deer, and bears. Their religion, called *Washat*, teaches that "God gave us these things for our use." Before they go into the hills to gather roots that burgeon in the spring or berries that ripen in the summer, they hold religious ceremonies in the long houses at Satus and White Swan. These are their times of thanksgiving. They know that man is but a part of nature's pattern, that from nature comes man's bodily sustenance and his spirit's strength. Without such knowledge any man must live and die palely, half-conscious.

I am as grateful for having known their philosophy as for having known Mister B. In memory I put spring's first salmonberries into my hand, holding it down for him; and he gobbles them up, sliding his v-shaped underjaw into my hand, rummaging around with his tongue for spilled juice, then badgering at my leg for another handful, grabbing with his forepaws onto my jeans and looking up in perfect trust. "We are God's creatures, you and I," he told me, "equally."

XII *Rabelaisian Bear*

Life was Mister B.'s carnival. Although he had had his traumatic moments, particularly when his own mother rejected him (and this still showed in the fact that he could not stand to be rejected by his mother-substitutes), for the most part, life to him was a gaily colored beach ball. He took obvious delight in everything he did: eating, sleeping, nature-study, tree-jousting, bathing. And in "baiting" his associates, both human and animal.

I had known that bears are humorists of a gross, robust type—but not at close range. My earlier education came from films taken by Lois and Herb Crisler during the decade they lived at Humes Ranch, inside Washington State's Olympic National Park. During that time, from 1941 until the early 1950s, they spent summers (and some of their winters, too) in the Olympic High Country. One fruit of their hardships and skill is *The Olympic Elk*, a Disney True-Life Adventure release.

In Crislers' films I had seen black bears (the only kind found in the Olympics, or in Washington State, now that the grizzlies are gone) at play. From a distance, undetected, Herb Crisler had captured the bears at a private game, sliding down snowbanks. Follow-the-leader style, the bears made a running start from the top of a snowfield and went belly-whopping down, sometimes turning somersaults, sometimes just tobogganing on their bellies. For pure delight!

The sawdust pile by the horse barn was Mister B.'s lowland snowbank. He breast-stroked up to the top, then took a jump and slid down. It was "slower" than snow, but he loved it. When sledding was over, he pawed the sawdust with both forepaws into a mound under his belly, then lay on his back in it, rolling back and forth or over and over. Sawdust speckled his hair, like cleaning dust in a deep-pile rug. He buried his snout in the clean, pungent stuff fresh from the sawmill; he tumbled, snorted, and coughed. It was not as daring as leaping off a snow cornice or thrusting out and down from the top of a snow slide in the High Olympics, but it was pure fun. He made a "whooof" of joy as he launched himself out for each slide-down.

The creek was always a part of his carnival. On hot summer days Nameless, the dog who had discovered him and who remained his favorite playtime companion, would frequently lead him into the cool shallows of the creek crossing. There she would gambol around and around, while Mister B. did his best to follow, occasionally rearing to whop the water with his huge forepaws. Then he would whirl and stand up before her, dripping, as if asking her to box with wet gloves. She gave him a sneer of maternal indulgence or a snarl of adult outrage, and he dropped to all fours to cavort some more.

He often played with the four adult dogs, Nameless in particular, long after their capacity for playfulness had run out, so that he would visibly bother them at last. They would turn on him, lips drawn back in a subvocal growl (probably audible to *him*), and still he would stand up, putting his big forepaws on their backs or heads. They would have to shake him off and leave the scene. There was no "enduring" him and his capacity for continued horseplay in their more sedate scheme.

This "fun" was why he would turn and whirl on them while they were engaged in the serious chore of following me down the woods roads or scenting rabbit tracks. It upset their forward motion and he took a bearish delight in doing so.

When they would no longer tolerate him in the creek, a frenzied humor pervaded his ballet with creekside trees. He leaped at a tender-barked alder, grasping it about four feet up, and hoisted his dripping body speedily toward its top. When he got to where the tree began to bend with his weight, he took a firm stance on a limb with one hind foot, grabbed the main trunk with his teeth, and shook, scratched, and wrenched in a fit of healthy exuberance. When the bark was well slashed and some of the upper limbs leaned down awry, never to grow straight again, he came slicing down, rushed to another tree, and leaped to do his swashbuckling bit all over again. To this day, the bark-slashed, weird-limbed alders by the creek say: "Mister B. had fun here."

The bushes of the house yard likewise knew the ecstatic ravages of a bear on a tear. He climbed into the white lilac bush, splitting it at the forks; he wrenched the honeysuckle bush; the mountain ash knew his midnight madness when, like a small boy, he climbed it toward the full moon. Unlike a boy, he mouthed and gummed the smaller limbs while his hind legs ripped and tore at the limbs he stood upon. It was like a silent, demoniac laughter of the entire body.

He loved to contact all living things, as well as trees—

[18] *He liked to "help" with chores by climbing out on the barn rafters to supervise whatever was going on.*

[19] *In October he had a glistening coat, a lordly air. He felt that he owned the world.*

[20] *The creek was still a place of fun and wonder.*

[21] *He would dash circles around one of his playmates, then suddenly stand up and tower over him.*

[22] *Mister B. up his favorite tree, a maple outside the cabin's west windows. This is one of the last pictures of him.*

loved to be rippled, tickled, patted, and mauled; loved to have his foot-soles examined, to s-t-r-e-t-c-h his toes as I held his paw from behind, in the pad of my own hand. As he gained weight and got longer (or taller), he took pleasure in having Bill "box" with him, play-biting or cuffing his human opponent's fists.

Bill enjoyed it, too. When we were first here, we spent many days exploring the surrounding mountains. One day, along the rim of the creek about half a mile up, we heard a noise like that of a small army marching through the brush. Walking forward through the small trees we saw an adult bear, standing upright beside an eight-foot fir stump, wrenching the bark away to get at grubs or ants. The noise of his industry filled the otherwise calm morning.

"I'm going down and wrestle him," Bill said. (The Davy Crockett influence?)

"I'll watch," I replied.

But when we got within challenging distance, the bear took one startled look, dropped to all fours, and went puffing and snorting away uphill, as loud, almost, as a locomotive. But faster. When he got to a log across a ravine and was halfway along it, a safe distance, he relieved himself and continued on uphill.

Bill had remained unsatisfied in his ambition to bear-wrestle, and I could see that he hoped to someday find a reasonably adept opponent in Mister B. They were both, obviously, training for it; and it seemed to me that, with the way things were going, Mister B. might well, within another year or so, have the last laugh. In the meantime, it was part of his fun.

He found amusement even in rolling rocks. Here, again, he had boundless opportunities for simple pleasures, for this land, called "gravelly loam" on the land maps when we bought it, is the moraine left by glaciers which were whole hills deep, so that to start a gravel plant, as some of the pioneer families have, one merely builds a bunker against a steep hillside and lets-'er-roll. No one is deeply concerned about hauling the dirt washed from the gravel and sand away: there isn't much—just a coloring, a muddy shading of the wash water.

When rocks, trees, water, wrestling, and animals wore out as sources of amusement, Mister B. haunted humans.

A neighbor lady had, as long-term house guest, a girl who had spent her late teens in a nearby city. At home among urban sophisticates, she had left behind the innocent delights of a childhood shared with her grandmother who had gathered herbs and sold them. When the girl told me of this occupation, she did so with depreciation for her grandmother's simplicity. "And it was such hard work!" she said.

"Hard work" and "satisfaction" were antonyms, to her; a person who toiled under the sky, in sunlight or rain, could not possibly be happy, she thought. She had preferred to "live by her wits" in the city's web.

Her viewpoint seemed obscene to me. But Mister B., who sensed her fright of inhuman animals, turned the tide. He would chase her into the house. When she latched the screen door, he clawed at the edges until he loosened the screen and made a hole he could wedge through.

Then she had no recourse but to lock the solid doors and look out. But the front picture windows went nearly to ground level and so Mister B. stood up and put his paws flat upon them and mashed his nose against them, fixing her with a glare which was actually one of nearsightedness, but which she took to be personal censure. She shrieked. At this, Mister B. would beat upon the windows with his fore-paws until the panes undulated like the sinister ground-swells of a rolling sea.

Into the inner bedroom she dove, and locked that door. She emerged later to get her radio and, the coast looking clear, sat down again in the front room to hearken to rock-n-roll and polish off a plate of spaghetti. But no sooner had the inside movement begun (she slid about, cautiously) than the pounding resumed, for Mister B. had not left the amusement park; he had merely taken a nap in the flower bed under the window ledge.

Up jumped the devil.

"Save me," squealed Eve.

Still full of fun, Mister B. shinnied the fir tree at the house corner and appeared upon the roof. First, he dug under the asbestos shingles over the front hallway, just be-hind and beyond the door, and his earnest endeavors brought him down to the two-inch planks which underlay the roof-ing. That did not help him (nor me, either, for the roof leaked at that spot forever after, and I was called upon to remedy his ravages after every rainstorm).

Finding solid impenetrability there, he went over the roof-top, walking the roof peak for a while like a carpenter sur-veying a finished job, and thence down to the bedroom where she lurked. He "dug" there, too, while she, cowering beneath, got under the covers and turned up the volume.

He went after her in the summer berry patches, too, but she always had her hostess along then—a lady who talked without restraint to Mister B., as to a "disturbed" child: "Get away, bad bear!"

And Mister B., turning away with maddening deliberation, answered in kind: *Nyawwwwww,* with left foot raised and head reared backward, fangs exposed.

His bearish joshing seemed to me to be a most therapeutic treatment for the girl, and I thought that had she had more of it, she might have been retrained, in time, to a knowledge of her own proper place in nature.

Only once, when he had sneaked into the house to haunt her, did Mister B. leave of his own volition, and precipitously.

The neighbor lady belonged to the hospital-visiting committee of Seattle's Indian Center. Sometimes she brought paraplegic patients home to visit on holidays and weekends. Once, when a man of the Swinomish tribe was sitting in his wheel chair in her front room, silently smiling into space, Mister B. clawed the edge of the screen door and found it unlatched. He stalked in boldly to perpetrate his scare.

All of a sudden he became aware of the stranger. He looked at the Swinomish man. The Swinomish man (than whom there never was on earth a more peaceable soul) looked back at him.

Mister B. turned stub tail and *ran.* The screen door chattered at his passing.

The man chuckled in his throat as he told me, afterward: "He got out of there like the devil was after him." He thought for a space, and added: "He probably thought I was his father!"

He showed me no such filial respect. He never lost the habit, no matter how large he grew, of horseplay at my expense. For the pure fun of it, he would fall into step behind me, make a sudden sprint, rush up and grab my leg from behind, giving a sideways bite that went through the jeans; then he would let go equally abruptly, rush around and ahead, looking back with a devilish gleam.

Leg-grabbing was something he tried only on friends. Strangers were for climbing and nuzzling, if they allowed it, but "bite and run" he reserved for intimates.

Life's most casual happenings gave him pleasure. When he was allowed inside the cabin, he did not merely walk in, he grabbed the door jamb with his front paws and swung himself inside.

When he lay on the front-room floor, one could *see* him enjoying life: quirking his ears to the sounds of baby chicks outside, down below the garage; lifting his nose toward the "echo sound" of a second brood of baby swallows overhead, where the birds had come in through a knothole and nested above the ceiling. He attended with his whole being when something got out-of-rhythm, like the sudden quick skittering of chipmunks on the top side of the ceiling as they rushed and thrust after some of the winged maple seeds they had been storing away and, suddenly, in animal funship, had stopped to play with. They did this unpredictably, out of tearing high spirits, as if they had "the winter bit" well licked and could afford to grasshopper for a while in the midst of their serious occupations.

Their frolic seemed reflected in his own sense of well-being. I wonder why we do not see this more often in the human animal—this pausing in the midst of harvesting (whether of crops or money or thoughts) for a time of pure joy. Is it the Puritan in us? or are we simply too far removed from the spontaneity of being an honest animal? Probably Europeans in their harvest dances have this "relief" from work. Certainly our own Indians possess it still, albeit muddied and muddled. But I have seldom seen an

American or a group of them drop work to really *play*. They "take" vacations, only they work at it, as if they were taking medicine.

Mister B. never had to force himself to enjoy life. He walked to music as all wild creatures do, and some persons, too. Thoreau's "different drummer" he certainly heard. And he did his own bit of musical composition: claw marks up the door and on green-barked trees throughout the woods are, to this day, the notes of his music; the limbs of plum and berry-bearing trees, slanted earthward, his bars, irregularly spaced.

He wrote with all four paws, diligently. It was not all joyous and lyrical music by any means, for when the ever serious problem of food was posed, he screeched "beware!" to other aspirants at his trough; and when he was dislodged from human contact, he moaned a warning: "You'll be sorry if you reject me." But, given the basics of food and warm companionship, the rest of life was all powdered sugar on his blackberries: a gambol in the creek, a wrenching ballet with a tree, shadow boxing with the dogs, and play-biting me.

Because he was always well fed and securely companioned, his sense of humor had space in which to develop fully in all its nuances. He never had to wonder about whose world this is: he knew it was *his*. He lay on his back and juggled it in the air with all four feet, snorting hoarsely and grinning for pure joy.

XIII *Wild Animals Are Individuals*

Mister B. was like a living book, with new secrets for me to learn each day. One of the most startling things concerned his range of emotion and his maturation personality-wise. I had thought bears to be "all of a piece," as much a chunk or lump of emotion on the inside as they appeared to be on the outside at first glance—although even in appearance they had vast individual differences when studied closely. The dictionary said: "bear. 3. A surly, uncouth, or morose person"—certainly, I found, an abridged definition.

Whoever heard of Smokey the Bear reverting to infanthood and nuzzling a ranger's arm? Or picking up his shovel and flinging it in a tantrum? Or baring his teeth and snapping in pique when the cameraman moved on to another assignment? Or standing up and whirling before a horse to "spook" him, then rushing down the field ahead of him: "Come on, let's *see* who's faster!"

He grew up, as a child does, erratically: precocious in some ways, backward in others. He became quite independent about where he slept and whether or not he ran toward humans when they passed him on a dozing-stump. Yet, when he did come to his friends, he continued his fits of nuzzling and dry-nursing, making himself look ridiculous to strangers as he clambered, even when two-thirds my weight, up my torso to go mmmm-mim-mumm at my neck.

Through association with many humans he developed a well-rounded personality, so that he could interpret human voices and gestures. He could discriminate between friends and casual observers, children and adults, those who would stand for horseplay and those who would not. He had distinct personal likes and dislikes; those who, he knew, regarded him as merely a delinquent type were on his black list; those who admired and respected his complexity of character and who expected great things of him he outdid himself for.

In matters of learning he matured. One dark night I went down to a neighbor's house. He rushed after me, running headlong into one of the granite boulders which I had placed along the lower edge of the yard. "Whack!" I heard his head hit the rock. "*Waah!*" he yelped at the sudden pain.

But instead of rushing to me and bawling to be soothed, he took it upon himself, as an adult, to solve the problem. When I returned to my own house shortly thereafter, he was going in and out through the rock fence, learning the trail. He ran after me in the dark other times but he never thereafter collided with a rock.

He taught himself to put survival above mere companionship, so that he could allow me to leave a berry field without his having to follow. He could stay there picking by himself for another hour or all afternoon.

Through his relationships he had advantages for higher

education, but I believe that he was also *individually* precocious, learning more quickly and more fully than many another bear individual might have.

Men belong to the human family, but each has his individual differences. Animals, too, are individuals. In acting out their lives they seldom run true to the mass patterns set down for them in textbooks and folklore. Size, form, so-called behavior patterns, and even bodily necessity sometimes have little to do with the way individual animals—or pairs or groups of animals—actually *do* perform.

Consider the swallows. A few seasons ago we had barn swallows in the garage for the first time. A highly vocal, seemingly youthful pair, they discussed each move—particularly the laying of the fifth egg in their first nest—at length. Also, they were the first swallows I've known that wouldn't build a large enough nest.

For several days their nest was a mere ridge of mud along a narrow lip of shingle protruding near the top of a supporting post in the garage. I poured water in the driveway in order to manufacture mud for them; they took it and started a nest on the large metal cover of the overhead light. The space was ample, but the nest was too small. Their first five eggs hatched; by the sixth day the birdlings were overcrowded; that night they all jumped or were pushed out and died—half-naked, large-winged—some on the garage floor, some on the workbench.

The birds rebuilt on their original shingle. The nest flared outward but still they could not bring themselves to build spaciously. They continued to quibble over every drop of mud and each tiny feather for the lining. The hen swallow had literally to stand up in the nest in order to lay.

She could not sit down to incubate, either, and finally,

after all the other barn swallows had gone to the valley below to congregate for migration, our pair left—deserting the three eggs in their second clutch. I opened one: it had not begun to develop, for the swallow couldn't get down into the nest to warm it. I had thought that birds had an instinct for all such things, but this pair didn't. Nor did they appear to learn through trial and error.

Individual animal differences don't necessarily bring tragedy. One humid June day I met a birdling that refused to be hypnotized—a saving trait. It was a baby song sparrow, stub-tailed, just out of the nest. Its squawking attracted me. It balanced on a log in the swamp, on legs like black toothpicks. Behind it on the log stretched the largest, alertest, hungriest-looking garter snake I have seen—one about thirty inches long and heavy of girth. It must have seemed a boa constrictor to the bird, with eyes like slitted locomotive headlamps.

There's a dead fledgling, I thought, but the bird did an unnatural thing. Refusing to be mesmerized, it flew directly down the length of the serpent, lighted on the log at its rear, and pecked the very end of the black reptile tail where it thinned to worm size. It was one of the heartwarming minor incidents which have proved to me, during the past twenty years on this ranch, that animals, too, are individuals.

Whole groups of birds may act in ways they "shouldn't." There have been four to seven Canada, or gray, jays, commonly called "camp robbers," living among the hemlock and Douglas-fir groves ever since we purchased these 160 acres. They wouldn't do as they are supposed to—come to us and beg or filch food. It took twelve years before they came down to us from the treetops. Although camp robbers are supposed to parachute into camp the moment bacon is sliced or a hotcake flipped over an open fire, ours didn't. They floated down one autumn, every pinion feather clearly silhouetted against the sky and muttering their plaintive calls, and haunted the chicken yard where young fryers were developing. It was a sort of autumnal aberration. It lasted just a few weeks and then the camp robbers took to the treetops again. Apparently they had higher tastes.

My parents, lifelong Audubon Society members, visited here in late September, 1958. Looking out of the front window in the morning, my father was intrigued by actions of the Oregon juncos—black-cowled, pinkish-beaked "snowbirds" that flock here the year around. The juncos were chasing insects—rushing up in zigzag spurts, hovering, darting, jerking up and down on individual strings to which the insects seemed attached and catching them on the wing.

"That's the first time I've seen juncos acting like flycatchers," Dad said.

To me it was nothing unusual; they act that way here all the time. Life is tougher on Tiger Mountain; perhaps that's why new habits are developed at times.

There are wild animals in these foothills of the Cascade Mountains that are large and far from helpless. That does not mean that they are forever acting out the law of the fang and the claw. It all depends upon their individual natures.

The bear that Bill and I had come upon up the creek canyon one May as it was clawing bark from a fir stump outweighed us by several hundred pounds, but he had not wanted to attack. Some counties of Washington State have an open season the year around on bears, classifying them as predators. We have found the several individual bears we have known to be predatory only on ants, grubs, wild blackberries, and skunk-cabbage roots.

It was July when I met the timid bear again, this time in a deserted orchard up the road. After chores one near-dark day I had hiked up with a gunny sack to get some Yellow Transparent apples. I crossed the pasture, where a neighboring rancher's cattle grazed, and went into the darkened grove. Under the Transparent tree I made out a fat, black form: a Holstein heifer, I thought, that had strayed from the other cattle.

"Sooo boss," I said.

The "heifer" bolted forward and hit the barbed-wire fence on the orchard's far side. Wire and posts screeched and staples popped. Then the bear backed off, leaped the fence, and I could hear it snorting and complaining with fright in the bracken patches beyond. We have since met Tiger Mountain black bears that are much less timid, but this one was being true to its own individual nature.

Because of such meetings, when neither bears nor humans knew the other or what to expect of the other, we learned that animals are not as they are pictured in gossip and fable. A Pacific Northwest fictionalist has climaxed many of his outdoor tales with the fight that is his classic: it's between a bear and a cougar and it's to the death. That isn't the way our real bears—the timid one and the others—would do it. Nor would the cougar cooperate.

Herb and Lois Crisler, while living on Humes Ranch in Olympic National Park, saw cougar "signs" several times. Once Lois found the spot where a cougar had crouched in snow on the root-cellar roof while she had gone there for canned goods the night before—and realized why she had felt "the hackles rise" on her neck in the dark. The cougar that Cris finally met face-to-face merely wanted to play.

Cris used to carry wheelbarrow-loads of bark from the forest to the Humes' cabin. One evening when the snow was deep, he entered the gate of the picket fence he had built to keep deer and elk from the garden, and was starting for the house when a cougar appeared, almost magically, between him and the front porch.

"He stood there, swishin' his tail. Then he pounced back and forth like a big tabby cat worryin' a mouse. I was too surprised to move. I called to Lois," Cris said, "then I just waited."

He had straps on his shoulders to balance the load, and there didn't seem to be much he could do *but* wait. Would Lois come in time? Could she help? Would the mountain lion with its muscular shoulders, thick neck, and bright yellow eyes attack?

The cougar waited in front of Cris for what seemed infinity, belly-crouched, tail twitching. Finally, he leaped, but he leaped over and away! He seemed to float past Cris's lee side and off into the gloomy forest. "Then it came to me," Cris said. "He had been wantin' to play."

Thus an individual cougar may be the antithesis of the bloodthirsty killer of American folklore. Another public myth about wild animals, which individuals do not bear out, is that they are stealthy creatures. Deer are supposed to filter noiselessly through vine-maple thickets; bobcats are said to move at night as tawny shadows gliding through deep glades. Those who live with the wild ones know that they are *not* members of some mountainside silent service.

A deer I reared could be silent while he was lying in a thicket, chewing his cud, daydreaming, but when he leaped up to come to the house for a handout, he made a noise like a herd of water buffaloes in a jungle of brittle-stemmed bushes.

Wild deer are also often noisy. They stand on their hind hoofs, get a good purchase with their teeth on the branches of apple or cherry trees—particularly when the fruit is ripe— and jerk down the lower boughs. On a summer evening, in the vicinity of a deer-thronged orchard, the sounds of their tree-grazing are anything but muted. When alarmed, deer sometimes move away in four-footed bounds, the thumps diminishing off through a bracken field. Often enough, when they are running or even merely grazing through thickets, they snap dead sticks and limbs loudly. I have gone toward the sounds of what I supposed to be grazing cattle and found them to be deer.

Bobcats are sometimes different, too. A neighbor down the Tiger Mountain Road found a bobcat kitten and brought it home. It did not sleep all day and slither forth at night. He was active in the day, and when he grew older, would break the chicken-wire mesh of his cage and take off right down the center of the road, swaggering, not slinking, his stub tail jerking cockily from side to side. There was nothing stealthy, or even particularly catlike, about his movements. He *stomped* along, on straight, decisive limbs. Likewise, the bobcat I saw stepping along solid rock by our waterfalls one winter moved over the snow not with feline craftiness but in a matter-of-fact, long-legged way.

Both the neighbor's bobcat and the deer I reared made plenty of noise and liked loud noises, or at least were attracted to them. Their wild compatriots, at least certain individuals, have the same sort of reaction.

Tom Spaight, who has brought his bulldozers to our hill

land frequently, has said: "Lots of times deer come to the edge of a field or road I'm building in deep woods. They stand and watch, seeming to like the bulldozer noise."

Animal tastes, too, are not what we think they "should be" around bulldozers. Spaight said that when he leaves his dozer in the woods he sometimes returns early the following morning to find deer licking grease from the fittings or tonguing a gasoline can. "The first time it happened I was surprised, but after that I expected it," he remarked. "There must be some mineral in the grease that they have a taste for."

Tiger Mountain coyotes likewise have unusual eating habits. Our particular coyotes do not make raids on the poultry but rather on small, round Indian plums and fallen apples in the orchard, carrots and pumpkins in the garden, grass and old mountain-beaver skeletons in the woods. We had goats which roamed the mountain each day for several years accompanied only by a small dog, but coyotes never touched them. Once something killed a milk goat each of three days in a row and a kid the fourth day, but the killer turned out to be a stray dog. Our coyotes are not rapacious meat-eaters, except in the realm of mice, grasshoppers, and beetles. They are often vegetarians.

Eating habits with many animals hinge upon their powers of preserving food, and individuals don't always do what they "should" in this regard. Above our slanting field lives a particular mountain beaver that—of dozens of his compatriots here—won't lay away hay for winter in the underground storehouse which he should use. He just keeps cutting his greens all winter long, using whatever he can find as the weather changes: the last, low fireweeds in October; a few thistles after the first freeze; sword ferns and blackberry leaves during the wet winter months when there are no other greens. When these are covered with snow he climbs short cedar trees to gnaw off and bring down the branches. He probably suffers many an underground stomach-ache from munching chill boughs full of cedar oil, but year after year he repeats his performance of individual improvidence.

On the other hand, some wildlings are too provident. A friend of mine owns part of an ancient railroad right-of-way on Windy Mountain, near the summit of Stevens Pass in the northern Cascades. The railroad ties have been taken up; the one-time boom towns of Korea, Nippon, and Tokyo are now just dots on the map and grassy patches on the mountain. But the huge, riprap bulkheads, built of ten-by-fourteen-inch timbers with a fretwork of openings, remain. These bulkheads held the talus slopes from sliding onto the tracks.

In these openings the conies or rock rabbits have stored hay. On Windy Mountain the pikas are no pikers. They have forced grass and leaf hay into the bulkhead openings until it cannot be stuffed further—so tightly that a man cannot budge it with his fists. It is as if some push-button of providence were pressed and they went on stuffing provender into the haymows which were provided, simply because the openings are there.

Wild animals have similar habits of an individual nature where their built-in capacities for self-defense are concerned. My four-year-old niece, Linda, came with her family to live nearby on Tiger Mountain. One of her special pets was a lizard—the lizard that wouldn't drop its tail. Some species of lizards are supposed, when captured, to rustle away, leaving the last segment of their tail, which breaks off neatly in the middle of a vertebra, in the claw or maw of their assailant. But not Linda's lizard. It clung to her sweater as a brooch, curled in her hands, lived in a bottle in the basement or under a rock outside the basement door. It was quite willing to be captured anew, day after day, and happy, apparently, to keep its tail intact, although other individuals of its species did not do so.

One July afternoon I met the porcupine that didn't want to use his quills. I came upon him as he was licking a candy wrapper in the road. He stood up on all four feet, rattled to a roadside sapling, and climbed it to a height of about seven feet. There he clung, swishing his quilled tail vigorously to and fro in short jerks. When I put my hand near his tail it was obvious that he didn't want to stick me. He just looked down, in a mild-eyed, tentative way, and quit "swooshing" so vigorously. Later, I walked on up the road and he got ready to descend from his perch. A different individual porcupine might have shown more hostility.

My neighbor found a deer mouse floating in her sink one morning, clinging to the sponge. She washed the mouse gently, dried her off, and put her under a large glass mixing bowl, with a cloth to hide in. I kept the inverted glass dome on my writing table. The mouse with her pointed nose and glistering eyes came to know me. At last she would eat raspberries, seed by seed, while I worked. One morning I saw that the pink mouse foot was extended out under the bowl's rim. I stroked it with my finger tip.

The deer mouse drew her paw in, looked at it, then thrust it out again, to see if the alien contact would be repeated. It became a regular game, a line of communication between the small animal's world and that of the larger human one.

These experiences, among others, have shown me that

animals are as truly individualistic as are humans. Big-bodied, muscular men are sometimes timid; parents don't always know how to rear their young; some persons, embodied with a means of defense, use it cautiously or not at all. With humans, in times of great danger, curiosity, not an instinct for self-preservation, often prevails. Some are too provident; some, not enough. And the tiniest ones have unexpected bursts of good humor and come out of impossible situations, where danger should have overwhelmed them, safe and even singing.

It is the same with our wild neighbors.

XIV *Coming of Age*

When, in August, Mister B. came home for his evening meal as usual but then returned to the woods and stayed there by himself overnight, I realized, with that shock which comes to all parents in the normal course of events, that Junior was growing up!

For some time I had realized that he was coming of age, by fits and starts, as every growing youngster does, according to his own individual pattern: part latent development, part precociousness.

No longer a soft-nosed cub, and weighing in the seventies, he clambered my torso with a more significant weight ratio than formerly: we were about two to one, and he gained on me daily. He nuzzled, now, out of a sort of absent-mindedness or of long habit outwearing need. When dislodged, he no longer took it as a personal slur or insisted upon remaining. He merely looked aside, as if remembering a love affair of childhood, nostalgically but without passion, unclasped his claws, and dropped off to the ground.

It had become a performance by rote. He did it most often when there were other persons around, visitors, and then it was a sort of proof that *he* was still the King of the Mountain: "See, I have special privileges here."

Mister B.

He was getting so large it even embarrassed him a little to climb me; he preferred to stand up, resting his forearms on my arm or shoulder when I squatted to visit or knelt to weed, and making his nuzzling motions.

"The way he still does that, at his age, it's disgusting!" said Chuckie's mother, who had visited the ranch nearly every Sunday during the summer.

"But he can be easily discouraged," I replied. A nudge or stand-up, accompanied by "Act your age!" and Mister B. would let go, drop down, and move away making small nasal noises but without any of the traumatized bellowings of infancy. Indeed, after the first two months he had required much less neck and arm nuzzling. And at five or six months, he could easily be talked out of it.

Still, when nuzzling, he never lost the infant noise. His voice was deepening as his body grew and he was less vocal, but the nursing mmmm-mum-m-mimmm-mmm-mumm emerged with more volume but in the tones of infancy. I suppose that bears of two years or more may retain such sounds in the privacy of the family group.

He had a long infancy and adolescence as contrasted with his smaller neighbor animals: snakes, born to leave the mother's side within hours; Western bluebirds becoming so adult as to help their parents to feed the second brood of the season; young weasels and minks, leaving their mothers at three months or less. But bear cubs will stay with their mother through the first winter and sometimes through the second year. They continue to nudge and nuzzle and tussle with their mother long after she has ceased to give them anything but token sustenance.

Bears may continue gaining weight until the age of five. By August, Mister B.'s body had adult characteristics, as a human adolescent's does; but he would continue to put on weight for a comparatively much longer period than a human would.

His emotional patterns had been, at first, those of an "emotionally disturbed" child: "flat" and violently changeful, shifting from agony to satisfaction, scream to burble, in a second. He was easily affectionate, easily outraged. But there were almost daily, certainly weekly, changes toward independence and maturity that could be seen.

The changes could be noted even in his postures. When he reached four months, he began his "stalk." Sometimes, then, one of his usual easy-flowing or galloping gaits would cease abruptly and his legs would all get stiff as rigid cables with the feet attached at oblique angles, and he would move across the pasture grass with the robot jerkiness of a Frankenstein.

As an infant, he was protective of his underside, but then came the time when he felt secure enough to roll on his back, the several dozen scattered white hairs of his vest clearly visible, sometimes holding his favorite puppy in his arms, sometimes just lolling. To a friendly human stooping toward him, he would hold up one arm, unafraid.

At four to five months he began to stand upright a good deal and when a dog did something to bother him, would rise up before it, swinging his arms in miniature replica of an adult bear holding hounds at bay in a magazine illustration.

In infancy, when he snapped, yammered, and bit, there was no doubt of it: he was enraged and purely so, without reservations. As he matured in size and body movements, so did his emotions. He became more refined and complex, even in anger.

Mister B.

His behavior had nuances to match his emotions. In youth, perched atop a post, with the cow pawing the ground nearby, he bellowed with pure fright. In advancing age no emotion was that pure. He was always, then, looking out of the corner of his eye, as it were, like a human adult with *his* complex emotional webbing. Sometimes the look was, as with a person, a veiled consideration of things, an inner look. When he growled in his throat from under the cows' hay-feeder, he was also looking out slantwise to see where I was going next: should he follow his human friend or stay to torment his cow enemy? He might stop growling, perhaps even take a seven-winks nap under the feeder, then come forth, head up, mouth open: cow-oriented! Or, he might dash out from under the far end of the feeder to catch up with me. Or, he might go around the far side of the barn for a solitary expedition to the wild blackberries. Whichever he did, it was with a look aside, a consideration of what he might *otherwise* be doing. He even directed his snaps at the cow in a *sideways* manner.

Life, which is emotion in any living thing, was no longer A and Z to him, but a running together of the two, and all the letters in-between, and all those of the bear-alphabet to boot. And just as the emotional alphabet of the human has more symbols than the Chinese language, so Mister B. was becoming a rich layering, a *complex*.

This was most distinctly noted in his growing independence, his ability to make the choice to follow me or *not*. His staying apart was a little difficult for me to get used to, as it is difficult for a parent to alter his own pattern when the child reaches adolescence and then grows up and leaves home. It never reached the stage of my being glad when he was gone from home, but I suppose that it would have, in time, and thus have gone the full course of the parent-child relationship. The parent creature gets accustomed to being depended *upon,* just as the infant creature must have security *from* a provider (of food, which is to say, of love).

Now when Mister B. went out to the woods or swamps and stayed out, it was difficult not to go after him, wherever he might be, to see that he was out of harm's way; in effect, to tug him back to the shelter of long association. But there was also a heartening aspect in it, for I thought that he might soon become totally his own creature, returning to the wilds to stay. (But first came hunting season; and perhaps had he lived entirely through that, there would always have been some reason or season, on one side or the other, for him to remain close.)

Even in his manner of using his claws he matured. The points were like needles in infancy, and at first he had used them scratchily (and I surmised that his mother might have had such a case of scratched-chest that she had shunted him off rather than risk blood poisoning); and he had used them on my arms, back, legs and, even, once, eyes, so that I had to keep the covers tight around my neck while he was *in* the bed, or my head under the covers while he was *on* it.

But as he grew older and the claws grew huge and horny, until they looked like those on sacred Indian necklaces, he began to use them with more discretion; and by the time he was adolescent and the claws were capable of giving a good raking, he was not using them at all on his human or animal friends. Rather, he would lay his paw pad-flat upon my flanks, arms, or shoulders. If the claws hung up on threads of clothing, he would disengage them without ripping the fabric.

His entire disposition was settling, and he did not bite to hurt, either, but kept a gentle mouth, like a retriever.

Once when three-year-old Chuckie was sitting on a log in the front yard, facing the open door of the cabin, Mister B. came around the far corner of the house from one of his solitary woods-treks and ambled up behind the boy. When he got close, he made a small leap and placed his forepaws over Chuckie's shoulders from behind. Startled, Chuckie looked back, and up into the bright-eyed, lolling-tongued face hanging over his own small towhead.

He screeched! And broke into tears.

Mister B. fell back, mortified. "I wasn't going to hurt you," his posture said. "What are you trying to do? Make me out to be a monster?"

The boy, who had been his friend for several months, soon calmed down. But Mister B. never repeated that manner of surprise greeting with him.

I think that Mister B. matured in the reverse way, with age, from the panhandler bears in some of our national parks that get nastier and more impatient as they grow older. He surmounted original schizophrenia and became all-of-a-piece in his disposition: gentle and, while far from slothful, peaceable. And I think that it is true that animals, domestic or wild, reared by men, take on the personality characteristics of their fellow humans—just as animals reared in the wild possibly take on the very personality traits of their parents; and when they are in a situation with relatively mild and secure human beings, they become that way themselves.

National-park bears, around the camps and along the

highways, live a "what-happens-next?" life that Mister B. did not have to endure. They are "insecure" bears, perpetually meeting different personalities, loud voices, sudden movements, rejection-and-acceptance, all at once. Naturally they are unpredictable—as unpredictable as the humans whom they encounter daily in summertime. They are no more unpredictable than camera fiends such as the couple who, according to a friend who had worked in Yellowstone Park, smeared their small daughter's face with jam in order to get a picture of a bear licking it off. What the bear would do then *is* predictable; the people who would do such a thing *are not*.

Mister B. had never had to endure erratic inroads on his emotions or unexpected fits of acceptance-rejection from his friends. A consistent relationship made him develop an "easy," even trainable, character.

He was not supposed to come into the cabin except when invited inside, and he knew it. On a hot August afternoon he would lie by the front door, half in and half out, groaning as if he had a stomach-ache or making an open-mouthed, one-note moan and inching-inching inward. His purpose was to get into the front room and then to dart for cover in the cool ashes of the fireplace or under the desk or the davenport. He would s-t-r-e-t-c-h over the threshold, sprawled flat as a rug but with head up, eyes alert, trying to insinuate himself in without being seen.

He would finally get all the way in and lie out at full length on the cool hardwood floor, but just inside the door where a voice command or a flap of rolled paper could make him back out precipitously, only to commence his infiltration again.

We had chastised him with a piece of light molding strip,

about the size of a yardstick, and two of these paddlers had been laid down along the wall just inside the door. He held a personal resentment toward such sticks, apparently, and reached his nose in around the door frame and, taking them in his teeth one at a time, carefully dragged them out and deposited them in the yard.

"*Now* see what you can do to offend my dignity!" he seemed to be saying.

When the door was open and no one was in the room, he would appear silently as a shadow, pausing on the threshold, one paw lifted, to sniff and listen. Then he would make a *rush*, catercorner across the room to a far wall, to *under* something: the desk; the space between desk and bookcase; the bed; a pile of apple boxes full of clippings and old manuscripts. He would burrow his head into the dark corner, then turn around to peer out. He made such thrashings and crashings, seeking cover, that human hands usually reached in to remove him; then he snapped, snarled, and complained. Once in, he wanted to stay!

Although he did not actually bite and claw, as in infancy, he *looked* ferocious. He whirled about and snarled, mouth wide open, until he seemed as large as a Kodiak bear. Anyone who has had a ruffed-grouse hen come at him head-on down a woods trail, all puffed and screeching and tail pea-cocked, leaping with alarm, knows how a small animal can seem elephant-size. With a grouse or weasel or mink, motherhood-provoked does it; with Mister B. it was like masculinity-questioned in an adolescent lad.

If no one heard him enter, he would hide quiescently, but only for a while. Then he would edge his head and forepaws out (cobwebs embroidering his muzzle and shoulders), slide himself forward with his back feet pushing against the wall or floor, like a frog on the swamp's surface, lift his head and sniff for whatever food might be within raiding distance, for he never outgrew his compulsive-eating habit.

Two girls from the staff of a Seattle newspaper where I had once worked came to visit one September evening. While we were eating, Mister B. appeared and made his silent dash for under the desk. They watched in horror while I dislodged him and walked him to the door, fairly dribbling (the only time he ever did *that*) with rage and frustration.

"The next time we hear of you it will be under a head-line: 'Bear Kills Man,'" they said.

But I showed them my wrists: "Look, no teeth marks."

For he was never vicious, as a young man or a park bear may come to be, with rejection. He merely wanted to be sociable.

Like a teen-age boy, he developed concern for his appearance. In early youth his fur had often been matted here and there with fir pitch, stuck with straw (and then he looked like a bumpkin for sure), dusty with dried mud. But by early autumn he was careful to keep himself clean of foreign matter; he spent hours at a time combing and licking his fur until it shone.

And he preferred to sleep alone, recumbent on stumps or in cool, grassy places, as calmly as an infant who has never been hungry or a man who has never feared other men sufficiently to make him lock his doors at night. He slept right through the passing of hunters, who came through the gates with the No HUNTING signs—their rifles were their tickets of admission; they had learned reading, but not respecting.

Mister B.

He could doze atop a stump above the creek while I went by or while strangers passed, and no one who did not know where to look for him would even know that he was there. He did not *have* to be with me all the time, as formerly. He was beginning to be an individual, with the individual's need for a *margin* to his life.

I knew that it was necessary for me to learn to leave him alone, too, to respect his growing up just as a parent, if he or she is to avert tragedy, must allow a sixteen- or seventeen-year-old child the opportunity to *be* himself, must respect his individuality as long as the child respects the community. And Mister B. *did;* he was beginning to keep his own distance, and to allow others theirs.

It was not as difficult as I had thought it might be, this weaning of authority; and I was glad to look forward to the time when he would indeed be free of close association. It had not been possible when he was a cub, dependent for food and companionship, but I had always wanted it for him, and now it looked as if he could do the job for himself. Sometimes he could go all day without coming to the house, except morning and night for food.

He was becoming something better: a friend, not a dependent. He was not a leg weight any longer. A melancholy quality accompanied this development, but it was only for the wistfulness of youth's passing, which occurs as surely as do birth and death for anyone or anything, even a clover bloom or a blade of grass.

XV *Maple Tree*

Even casual visitors noticed the change which a growing sense of independence had wrought in Mister B.

Two high-school students, sons of Seattle friends, came to pitch their tent on a flat above the creek and camp there for the last few days before school reconvened in September. Mister B. regarded them from a distance.

"He followed along the creek while we were fishing," one said, "but he kept hidden. When we went toward him, he pretended to be picking berries."

His behavior, in that regard, was human. It reminded me of that of a young man who traveled cross-country, fully clothed, to visit a nudist camp located on a nearby mountainside: "I thought that if they discovered me in the shrubbery, I would pretend that I was lost," he said.

A week or so later Mister B. came back from the woods clothed in an impassive, disturbed silence. He ate, but he did not "talk," and he did not reach out for human contact. I could tell that he had had, and suffered ego-damage from, some wild encounter. There were no outward wounds or scars, but . . .

When a "delinquent" foster child returns from meeting

149

disturbed creatures of the ex-deformatory world at the Triple-XXX Barrel in a nearby town, one can tell from his talk that he *has* met them. He speaks an unspeakably vile language which reflects the horridness that he has remet. His words say, sometimes outright: "You don't know how *bad* I *am.*" One cannot say, then, that he *is* mean; but that he *feels* mean; and it goes against the natural grain of any young animal, the natural disposition which, while not all "sweetness and light," *is* goodness.

Or as when a child returns from grade school and you can tell by his whole manner that he has suffered a jolt: a hush has settled over him, a stillness of shock rather than of peace; he walks on the stilted legs of a terrifying insecurity. And sometimes you can tell, almost by looking, whether the shock comes from teacher encounter or other-children encounter or from the deepest heartbreak of all, betrayal by a bosom friend or a six-year-old sweetheart.

I could almost read Mister B.'s encounter, as if it had been written on his forehead; and I believe that it was with his Big Black Daddy or his Old Mean Mamma. For I could sense that it had been something big, but not human; something that had first attracted, then shocked without physically attacking him. But mostly, it was something that cannot be explained in a list of "reasons" a mile long but, like the encounter of the child returning, stilted, from school, something that makes a mark on the feelings: a hyphen, not a period (for life goes on and feelings, however bewildered, continue to have "feeling"). A definite stricture, a lash-stroke, a dash. Scar tissue. Hence, Mister B.'s stillness. He wished no reassurance here for a while, but left-aloneness in which to lick his inner wounds. He retreated to his maple tree beyond the cabin's west windows.

He had first taken to the tree, a giant soft-leaved maple, several weeks previously. At first he had dug a small hole in the turf on the north side of the house and tried lying on his back over that, but it wasn't cool enough. Up the maple, where even on hot days a breeze from the creek canyon stirs the canopy of hand-shaped, broad-fingered flat leaves, he discovered to be "just right." He snoozed or slept soundly for hours at a time in whatever crotch suited his growing girth. Sometimes he slept upright, hugging the main trunk. Sometimes his head and forepaws dangled over a horizontal limb while his bottom was wedged snugly into a Y-joint below and his back feet dangled. Sometimes his left hind foot and thigh were all that I could see from the typing table facing the windows, his trunk and forequarters being hidden.

Companioning him in the tree some afternoons were flycatchers. Cedar waxwings whirred to feed their young, perched on the topmost branches. A pair of black-backed, white-headed small woodpeckers rattled their Morse code on the several dead top branches that forked blue sky. A frost several Novembers back had killed them and, refusing to drop, they were white as skeleton shanks against the living green of the tree; at some places an orangish lichen growth splotched them.

In the September evening the Western stars were like bright fruit hanging among the boughs, perpetually revealed and rehidden as breezes moved the leaves. There, too, hung Mister B., like a furry fruit of a tropical tree, for several days and nights moving only to ease himself to a more comfortable seat, or to back slothfully downward for food and water. For the next two months, through September and

October, he did not ever quite regain his old quickness and temper. Or his pure joy of life.

He did become sociable again, but it was a slower-going manner that he had. Sometimes when humans came on Sundays to mill about beneath his tree and look up, he stirred, opened his eyes, and looked down, then slumbered again even before they had left.

Although I was concerned about the causes of his inactivity, I felt better about it when I had to take the mail route as substitute carrier. Then I could leave a dishpan of feed for him by the back door in the morning and be reasonably sure of finding him asleep in the tree when I returned in midafternoon.

One early morning I awoke to find that the power was off. Evidently a transformer on the pole near the house, a few feet south of the maple tree, had burned out. When I returned from the route that afternoon, the power company's repairman was parked in his pickup truck near the pole. He was talking excitedly into the truck's phone: "I can't go up that pole. There's a bear up a tree here and I don't dare get out of the truck!"

His wife had come along, and she sat beside him, her window rolled up, "smiling" a thin, straight line.

I reassured the man and he got out, to gaze up at the transformer; but he still would not climb the pole. Mister B., having recognized my car or voice, skinned down the maple tree and came to put his paws on my legs, then on the repairman's, in a conciliatory gesture. But his size, approaching ninety pounds, did not reassure the man, who leaped back into his cab. "I can't do anything here. I'll get a crew out to fix it tomorrow," he said, keeping a nervous eye on Mister B., who had decided to climb onto the back of the truck to take inventory of the tools and fixtures there.

The power was on again when I returned from work the following day. In the meantime Mister B., who was once again snoozing in his tree, had had an electrician's picnic.

"We came out with the big truck," one of the crew members, who returned with his wife and children to visit Mister B. on the following Sunday, told me. "The bear followed one of the men all the way up the pole. Then he came down and got into the cab and helped himself to a couple of lunches. When we got him out of there, he climbed onto the back of the truck. He re-sorted the insulators, tangled up the wire, and had himself a ball."

On a subsequent visit he told me that Mister B.'s day as a lineman's helper had been written up in their national trade magazine. He was going to send me a copy, but he never did.

At any rate, if Mister B. did not go forward as aggressively as formerly to meet life, life came to him, in his tree. All but the cats—they kept a haughty distance. But two red squirrels collected maple seeds there, passing *over, under,* around, and all but *through* him. Low-swooping birds drew chariots of autumn rain. A small house-bat came out from under the eaves to flutter past him at twilight. Above him the September nighthawks tipped and tilted and pole-vaulted upon their wing tips, scooping flying ants into their wide, bristle-bordered mouths. When the small rain came, a male robin sat above him, tail at a downward slant, like a shake on the roof. The woodpeckers continued to send their messages from the maple. Band-tailed pigeons, the last wild pigeons of our country, lighted, wings crashing, atop the ombu-like spread of the blue elderberry tree below the house. They feasted hugely, hovering their smoke-blue wings that so nearly matched the fruit for color, as they balanced upon the berry-clustered tips of the upper boughs. When Mister B. stirred, they kept their huge, mild eyes fixed upon him as they wrenched the fruit away by the beakful. When they left to return to the mountain, they lumbered up, making a noise like that of flying dinosaurs.

When there was nothing else to companion Mister B. in his tree, there was always the creek. The sound of the creek, muted, becomes the sound of rain, so that visitors walking into the cabin for the first time say, during a lull in conversation, "It's raining!" But, on looking out the west windows, they see sunlight dappling the dark, shiny-green leaves of the maple, deepening and darkening as evening comes, or as the season slides up the escalator toward autumn.

No, it is not rain. And so the creek is one's company, year long: willful and rampaging in floodtime; zizzing sibilantly under the snow; muted by summer's trees but like a small rain—the small-rain time being that of most comfort, for in the times of autumn's first rain one feels companioned even when this is not factually so. But even when children or a loved one are not present, there is a comfort in memory; and the catalyst for memory is the small, never ending rain-sound of the creek.

It was the comfortable sound Mister B. lived with. It was a time of waiting, yet of not waiting, for what one "knew" without daring to know *would* happen next. The tree was safe haven, for a season. It had been so since Mister B. first began to use it, since the time of his disturbing encounter on the mountainside beyond. "Be an umbrella to me," he told the tree. "Be what I can hold to safely, for this small time, at least."

Today, when I sit facing the window, I can see him in the mind's unwearied eye: snoozing, his hind feet dangling down in all security, as if earth itself were a safe harbor, with nothing to be feared by man or beast.

XVI *Not on a Chain*

When photographs of Mister B. came back in the mail from the developers, I showed some to "Steve," the Issaquah postmaster.

Steve smiled. "I remember when it used to be common to raise cubs around here," he said. "They had one on a chain down at one of the taverns."

A young man I knew had had, as a fourteen-year-old boy working for an Alaskan carnival, the keeping of a black-bear cub. "We fed him honey and oatmeal mush," he said. "As he got bigger, he got into so much devilment that we had to keep him on a chain. I was pretty skinny myself, and he grew so fast that when I had him out on the chain for exercise, we went whichever way *he* wanted to go and we didn't come back till *he* wanted to come. So once while we were traveling up to Anchorage from Seward, they decided to let him go."

Mister B. wasn't going to be chained. "The once-confined thing is never again free," Millay said; she was right, except in the case of a mink we reared: she *did* find real freedom after being caged. Most once-confined animals, including man, can never again be truly free.

There was a boy in our neighborhood who captured two young nighthawks. These strange, fork-tailed birds nest on the ground or, in cities, on graveled rooftops, and their two furry chicks are helpless until they feather out and learn to fly. He broke their wings, in order to keep them grounded. He lived on a hillside but his mind lived several stages down, for nighthawks' element is the upper air. They tilt incessantly upon the tips of their abruptly angled wings, then plummet earthward and at the bottom of their fall make a sound like a bull lowing from a distant field. They are called "bull bats," and the miracle of a bull in airy pastures should never be earth-tethered.

As far as movement went, there was nothing broken-winged about Mister B. Well-fed and properly respected at home, he still had the privilege and ability to leave whenever he wished to go rambling toward the mountain. He could sleep near home, or in any secret spot he chose. When he returned, there was always food, and friendly arms to mumble on, or a boxing session, if he liked.

Once he stayed out for two days and nights, and then returned, barging into the cabin, spurting toward me and standing up, all in a rush, to mumble on my upper arm. He weighed nearly a hundred pounds; when he stood up, his head reached to my upper arm.

When I happened to see him moving in the woods, alone, I noted that he went with the security of the fearless bumblebee thrumming on the late-blooming blackberry blossoms or in the last of the sun-stoked foxglove blooms. His security in the world was a far cry from the time in spring when we had tried to leave him on the mountain and had come upon him returning toward human home and "family," whuffling and snuffling to himself, all inner agony outwardly expressed, like a schoolboy beaten on the playfield the first day of school and chased home and finally, his pursuers leaving off, scuttling for home base as fast as he can, all panic and runny nose and squinted eyes.

Seeing him come home, *alive*, now in October, was shot through with the same sort of "relief" his earlier returns had brought. There was an urge to pick him up and to hide him in the "den" of encircling arms. Sometimes, when he returned, he would still be nearly as vocal as he had been in cubhood, indicating that the feeling was mutual.

He enjoyed the small scenes of remeeting. He had a terrific inborn sense of the dramatic. He was a natural actor, utilizing the dramatic effects which he could produce with two jetty eyes in a black face over a light-muzzled nose, a mouth the shape of that of an elephant, and a facile tongue. With these small elements, and his eloquent forepaws and voice, he could express all the emotions known to the veteran actor. With his eyes alone he could show hurt, amazement, slyness, shyness, coyness, belligerency, gratitude, dismay—the whole bag of tricks, one after another.

His eyes were particularly effective when he wanted something. High on his list were shock, chagrin, hurt feelings, and I need your help—like the carefully-studied coyness of a teen-ager "asking" for the car but, in reality, "demanding" it with every nuance of expression at his command.

So he clowned, and acted, and took to the woods through late September and early October. Autumn was his perfect time.

In the old garden he discovered the plum thicket that had grown from a single wild plum slip that I had planted years ago and whose sharp thorns had saved it from the livestock.

"Happy as a bear in a plum thicket." Thorn of the wild plum has torn my flesh reaching for the first white bloom of April, and for the round, blue fruit of early autumn, indicating, to me, that life's beauty and sweetness can also rend and tear. He knew how to take the barbs more gracefully than I ever had, or would.

From the plums it was a short trip to the creek crossing. He gamboled, making oval loops in the water; squatted, suddenly, up to his eyes, ears pointed; then plunged into a deeper pool or reached up for a bough of willow growing aslant the stream, and pulled it down, to sit in the water and meditatively tongue the furry-undersurfaced leaves.

Chuckie came to stay with me for a few days. The water at the fording place was at its lowest ebb, so that he and two other boys his age could squat on the sunny topsides of the stones and overturn them. Down underneath and in-between they found a fairy place, like the seashore when the tide is out. They found, first, salamanders, wet-skinned and shiny as obsidian. They found the nymphs of caddis flies, like square-jawed centipedes under the wet sides of rocks. They found trout, as tiny and perfect as jewels, and a shaggy-jawed bullhead.

Mister B. worked with them on this new frontier. All spring and summer they had all been crossing and fishing here; but this was the first time they had hunkered down and really gone at unearthing the underwater kingdom. Mister B. nosed the "sea life" without appetite. He may not even have recognized some of it as *life* at all.

But he had an insatiable, almost lustful delight in the turning of rocks. As the children turned them over, he would turn them back over, or over and over. Some he picked up in both paws; some he cupped in one paw, like a pitcher, and holding them along ground-level, bowled them.

If the children "shooed" him from a find, he might stand up to gape at them, then whirl down onto all four feet and rush to a bathing spot, or whirl and rush at a tree, leap into it, to rush aloft and tussle with it. He did not paw at the children, but he certainly wreaked havoc on the trees.

The world was his: he was never not "at home" in it. Any tree or creek spot or even lying-out-prone-place in the grass was his bank vault stuffed with gold, his guarantee of life and of earth's friendship.

Of one thing he was not free; he was tied to man, the enemy. A wild creature wildly reared has no built-in physical defense against the guns of man. But he does have the defenses of the meek: shyness, fear, retreat. His senses trigger these defenses: when he smells man, he flees. Being on his own ground helps. The thick underbrush and the hiding places which require a certain alertness to discover are his private allies. Autumn rain and the discomforts of walking where one cannot drive discourage his would-be killers.

But a wild creature reared to trust humans is quite as helpless as a sincere and honest human being dropped down into a reformatory of seven hundred two- or three-faced creatures without an element of conscience in their individual make-up. By character and training, then, he is a *victim*. There is no hope for him. What men commonly consider to be strong traits of character become his weaknesses. Through his own trustingness, he is betrayed. For trust will, under unnatural circumstances, destroy one—man or beast.

XVII *Death*

All of October was part of the open season on bears in King County. The season would close the first week of November. By the last week of October it seemed to me that Mister B. would live through.

Of course, his freedom had put me in chains. For when I could not see him, I could only hold, in one quarter of my mind, the target that would, eventually, catch the single shot meant for his heart, throat, or head. And the days, until dark closed down securely, I spent with almost a cessation of breathing, waiting to catch the hot rivet of lead. I could see him moving forward toward the raised gun, coming in peaceful greeting toward the human movement ahead of him . . . being, as he thought, a member of the family.

When in early autumn he had left on a voyage, before hunting season began, Bill had told me: "Make a cage of two-by-fours for him, in the barn."

Mister B. liked the barn. When I fed the cattle, he would often appear, suddenly and silently, a dark shape on one of the overhead timbers. Looking up, I would see the edges of his feet sticking out over the sides of the timbers. He walked like a man (or, a man walked like him), on the soles of his feet with heels touching the surface. The soles were large now, calloused and scratched with much traveling. I remembered when he had first come to us, how the foot soles had been smooth as a baby's, soft to the touch, and the fur edging them and between the toes and sole had been delicate, like a fringe of velvet appliquéd on.

If it was sundown, and the setting sun shining full on him, all the highlights of his coloring would show up: the glistering blue-black coat, relieved and pointed-up by the blond spots over each eye and the light hair of his muzzle that was not pure blond but brown-golden, with a light of its own. The brown hairs inside his ears had toned down in color as he got older. And there were a few pure-white hairs scattered across his chest and belly; they had been there since cubhood.

Looking up, I could see the sun showing pinkly through his inner nostrils. He yawned: his tongue was purple; the inside of his mouth clean and blood-pink.

His eyelashes were long, with several particularly prominent lashes at the inside corner of each eye. His eyes were perfectly round, like shiny marbles, with the white showing only occasionally; for the most part, the black iris filled the eye opening. His eyes were not as close together as on some black bears; the breadth of forehead and shagginess of hair made them seem closer together than they really were.

Every time I roused him from a nap there, I realized that I could build a cage for him in the barn till hunting season was over. Laziness did not keep me from it. Nor was it an "experiment" on my part, to see if he *could* live through hunting season. It was simply the feeling that he must be free to come and go, and that this was necessary *every day*, not just for ten months out of the year. I could not live caged, myself; I could not inflict caging on another, so closely human, creature.

Life, if it can be called anything but "existing," means freedom to come and go, to make decisions and to suffer or enjoy the fruits of those decisions. Most of all, of the many half-wild, half-domestic animals I have known, Mister B. craved that freedom. He loved to run across the creek-crossing logs at a gallop, his rear end up-humping as he scrambled forward and whizzed from the end of the last log and took off to the woods. He loved the textures of trees and their snoozing-places; enjoyed lifting his head to the chestnut-backed chickadees as they captured flying ants above him, or the red squirrels as they quarreled over maple seeds. He took a visible, paternal sort of delight in sharing the feeding troughs with growing calves or with a special, feisty bantam rooster who had been his lifelong friend. So, he went free.

The price of his freedom was, eventually, his death. The agony of an eventual, physical loss is *always* part of giving your heart, and if you cannot bear such agony, don't give your heart and don't give freedom—to yourself, or to anyone or anything outside yourself. Cowards don't. Cowards may "learn" without even trying. But the brave give their hearts eternally, over and over, in one degree or another. They give the deepest only once or twice a lifetime, but in the degree that they are capable of spreading and spending their loyalty and adoration, they give their hearts many times. From this experience comes an in-giving that is like the sea coming to land. But it does bring agony to higher land, too, for one cannot, being flesh and bone, also, lose physical contact without suffering the loss.

It is the nature of nature. All of it. The very grass in the high pasture springs, seeds, withers, and turns brown all in a few months; and then its life goes into the roots and new seeds until it springs to green and bloom again. The livestock passes over, browsing, nearsighted eyes askance when a strange shadow passes. They eat the grass and are nourished by it, the first green being not so strengthy as the later brown and raunchy seed-stuff.

But that passes, too, for eventually it is winter and there is no strength anywhere, save in the jagged-edged leaves of the wild blackberry. On these, I have known a cow to keep fat winter long; but one must find the correct sustenance; the incorrect will not do at all, and an unsavvy beast will starve, or must be coddled with soft hay.

When I had to be gone from the ranch, I worried about Mister B. above the other animals, as though for an errant child adrift somewhere upon the continental maze. But there was nothing I could *do*, physically, in either case— other than to think strong thoughts for the two of them—as strong as possible, between bouts of concern. In either case it was a cage and physical survival (like the keeping of hamburger in the deep freeze), or freedom of motion with the daily, hourly risk of some destruction. It was clean-cut with Mister B., for if he were not killed, he would undoubtedly survive, untraumatized and uninjured; but with the child, there were further complexities.

So "life went on." A retired seaman had insisted that I haul three thousand feet of one-by-six cedar boards for him to use in fencing his estate thirty miles to the north. That meant six trips with the pickup. I made them reluctantly, but by the time of the final trip, on October 26, I began to breathe freely; this one trip and I could stay home most of every day to keep an eye on Mister B. for the final few days of bear-hunting season.

I got up before dawn the day of the final haul. Mister B. was sleeping somewhere in the woods nearby. I left his breakfast for him by the back door of the cabin in a spot where the other animals would not get it: two pounds of dairy feed (the same as each cow got); three or four apples; and a dozen or so small, green tomatoes.

That will hold him, I thought; he will mess around the house, clawing on the doors and talking to be let in; then he will sleep in the front yard or play with the dogs, or go to the barn to "haunt" the cows and calves. By then I will be home.

It was still early morning as I drove back up the Tiger Mountain Road. Halfway between the old gate and the new one, on the road which had been hard-topped that year, I saw an arc of blood. I stopped. The blood was damp. I traced it back to where (directly beneath a NO HUNTING sign) the gob of blood was. One has to be at a butchering only once in a lifetime to know the throat blood's glob flushed from the slit gullet and congealed wetly.

Just there the knife went in—but probably he did not watch its jab-thrust from the human claw, undoubtedly being head- or heart-shot and unconscious. If he did see it, he knew—at the very last—that man can be betrayer as well as friend, seducer of life, death's black handmaiden.

The blood was still wet there, still wet in its arc on the road where he had been heel-dragged out from under the fence, as the line of crushed ferns showed.

There were bits of green tomato and dairy-feed pellets from his throat, on the road. Man had provided his last meal as well as his last agony on earth.

Mister B.

I tried to believe, at first, that it had been a deer, but it just wasn't so. And when I knew that he was surely gone, I thought of the things which should have been done and hadn't been. I had always "meant" to tape-record his voice; the voice was stilled. I had always "meant" to take color photographs of him; the color of life had left.

But the main thing was that he should have lived. As Macbeth said: "She should have lived hereafter; there would have been a time for such a word." It wasn't "to-morrow, and to-morrow, and to-morrow" that crept "in this petty pace from day to day"—but today and today and today. He was on the threshold of *becoming*: becoming an adult male bear, becoming a real test of whether or not an adult bear "turns on you," becoming an adult in his own right, a father of others.

Can one forgive one's self that this did not happen? In order to live, one *must*. There is only one thing that can be said: living, he enjoyed life; he was surrounded with love and trust (save for the two traumatic days or portions of days when his mother left him behind in the woods and went on with her other, better-loved cub or cubs). He was not betrayed, save in his feeling that *all* humans were friendly creatures. At the last moment he found that they were not. But it was only a moment, perhaps less than a moment, and so did not leave time, probably, for that saddening recognition of human betrayal at the very end.

He had a good, full life, *every day* (save only two) until the end. What more can anyone, man or beast, ask?

To this day his mementos are left. Going to feed the calves one morning recently, I saw for the first time a cedar-tree bough, bent down near the top, wrenched softly into an all-time downward curve, because of Mister B.

Coming back into the cabin, I faced the claw marks on the door, clear to the top, where he had stood on the door-knob and scratched to get in. As Lois Crisler, seeing them, said: "The claw marks remain."

The alders by the creek still know of his tree-ballets after swimming.

The animals he lived with survive. Stella, the little beagle-cocker wends her way here and there, a grown dog now, her belly only slightly out of shape from his mouthings when they slept together, both "pup" age, in the angle of the porch.

Chuckie, now five years old, went up through the woods a few days ago and I heard him telling his little brother: "Bears! Bears!" . . . without fright, as a small human animal *should* treat the subject.

The lilac bush split; the cherry tree crooked; the crab-apple lopsided; the mountain ash with one limb hanging down in an acute angle from the trunk—all say to me, the moment I open the door in the morning, "Mister B."

How fortunate above all humans are those who have *chores*, who work with the hands, daily, who have depend-ent upon them persons and creatures who must be cared for. For, in a time of agony, they *must* continue to live.

And now, when the moon walks in the house, down the lee side of midnight, and a white-crowned sparrow awakes to make one set of moon-washed trills (then tucks his head back under his wing), I can hear Mister B.'s brief claw-ing on the outer door just as realistically as I can hear the footsteps, returning, of one who cannot ever return.

For as long as blood is burning in one who remembers, no true experience is ever truly lost.